EVERY BLOKE'S A CHAMPION
EVEN YOU!

IAN 'WATTO' WATSON

WATTO BOOKS

A book by Watto Books

© Ian Watson 2012

Apart from any fair dealing for the purposes of private study, research, criticism or review as permitted under the Copyright Act, no part of this book may be reproduced by any process without the written permission of the publishers.

Some names are changed to protect the privacy of individuals.

Watto Books, PO Box 241, Woody Pt QLD 4019, Australia

ianwatto.com

ISBN: 978-0-9873788-0-4

Unless otherwise noted in the text, Scripture quotations are taken from the Contemporary English Version (CEV) © American Bible Society 1991, 1995.

Scripture quotations labelled NIV are taken from the HOLY BIBLE, NEW INTERNATIONAL VERSION® NIV®. Copyright © 1973, 1978, 1984 by Biblica, Inc.™. Used by permission of Biblica, Inc. ™. All rights reserved worldwide. "NIV" and "NEW INTERNATIONAL VERSION" are trademarks registered in the United States Patent and Trademark office by Biblica, Inc.™.

Scripture quotations marked (AMP) are taken from the Amplified Bible, Copyright © 1954, 1958, 1962, 1964, 1965, 1987 by The Lockman Foundation. Used by permission.

Scripture marked (NKJV) taken from the New King James Version. Copyright © 1982 by Thomas Nelson, Inc. Used by permission. All rights reserved.

Cover signwriting Chad Polinski

Cover design and internal illustrations Belinda Pollard

Reactions to
Every Bloke's a Champion... Even You!

There is only one Ian 'Watto' Watson, and there is no other book like this book. I believe *Every Bloke's A Champion... Even You!* has the potential to hit men like no other because of the wisdom, the clarity, the encouragement and the personal stories that bring it alive, but largely because of the unique language that will connect with ordinary men's hearts. You are a champion Watto and I love this book!!! Dr Fred Gollasch, Teacher/Educator/Amateur Concretor/Mentor/Co-founder of Better Blokes

Ian has been a fantastic friend and confidant for the past 30 years. **He has a wonderful knack for telling it how it is, which whilst sometimes confronting, is something most people actually enjoy.** I have no doubt his work in the community, especially his 'Shed' activities, have assisted many friends to enjoy their life much more than they might have otherwise if Watto had not been in their lives. Andrew Ireland, CEO Sydney Swans football club, former CEO Brisbane Lions

Ian Watson knows blokes. This bloke is very grateful for that! **Watto has taken a lot of listening, in truck cabs and pubs, in churches and around barbecues, and turned those years of experience into a few choice words.** This book is for you, champ, whoever and wherever you are. Phil Smith, Producer & Presenter ABC Radio 'Weekends with Phil'

In this book you will find pearls of wisdom from someone who has 'been there done that' and come through the other side on top. If you have 'been there done that' and yet to come through the other side, take heed of the wisdom before you. **If Watto can do it, believe me 'so can you, no matter what'.** Be encouraged to go forward and become a Champion Bloke. Chris Modlin, Business Consultant

Every Bloke's A Champion... Even You! by Ian 'Watto' Watson contains straight shooting, down to earth, honest to goodness 'pearls' every bloke will benefit from reading, pausing and applying. **Whether it be about anger, sex, generosity, relationships, or connecting with the Big Fella on a first-name basis, this book shines light on the roadway us blokes are travellin' on.** Thank God for one of the older fellas taking the time to record their lessons from the school of hard knocks and being willing to pass on such pearls to the rest of us. We will do well to take stock from the scares, tears, trials and successes of this elder statesman. It gives me strength to continue to take risks knowing I'm part of the tribe of men who can listen to, speak to and call Ian, 'friend and brother'.
Michael Knight, Peer Power, Co-Author *Being a Bloke*

Watto is a champion of champions. He is an honest bloke who has not only learned from making mistakes but wants every bloke to reach his potential without making the same mistakes. His heart is bigger than the MCG, his passion for men outweighs his love for footy and it is a pleasure to have him as an authentic mate. **Fellas, listen to what Ian 'Watto' Watson has to say. He will encourage your heart and put a fire in your belly so that you can live life as a champion!**
Peter Janetzki, Host of Talking Life 96five Brisbane, Counsellor & Educator, Co-Author *Being a Bloke*

This book is possibly one of the most important how-to books I've ever read (excluding the Bible). I can think of so many people that I could give this book to. The empathy, genuine concern and humbleness from the author are just so terrific to hear. Growing up with very little encouragement from my father, basically believing I wouldn't amount to anything, **the male encouragement explained in this book might have saved me so many years of frustration and negativity.** I might have realised my dreams much earlier. Warren Evans, Property Consultant

When you hear Watto speak, you feel like you are in the sheds at half-time listening to an old-style footy coach revving you up for the next half. You would go out and run over dead bodies in **pursuit of victory.** Watto writes as he speaks as he is. He encourages, coaxes, urges you to have a good look at yourself and be the 'real deal'. He finds his purpose through a relationship with the 'Bloke Upstairs', but whether you want this path or not, this is a book for blokes who feel an emptiness inside and have tried every possible way to deal with it. Years of experience give Watto wisdom worth passing on. For blokes, and for anybody for that matter, let the coach look you in the eye and lovingly share some half-time truths. There's some winning to be done! Jim Strelan, Pastor

Watto writes like he lives – straight up, passionate and about as ridgy didge as you can get. **This book is written from real life experience in a language the average punter can understand with stories we can relate to.** Have you ever battled with life & love or just questioned how spirituality and the Big Fella have any relevance to today? This book is a must read for every Aussie bloke! It will fuel your heart and stir your faith – just like my mate Watto does every time I encounter him! Paul Morrison, West Coast Eagles football club Chaplain, Shed Happens WA

Touching and transforming lives in a positive way doesn't happen overnight, and in Watto's case his work has been mastered over decades. **I can best sum up Watto by saying he oozes a passion and genuineness more of us need to experience. Every bloke deserves to hear the message of this book.** Peter Dutton, Federal MP

Who would have thought, that a truck driving trainer could write such an **inspirational, down to earth book, that deals with the nuts and bolts of life**! I am not a big reader, but I found it very hard to put down. You are an inspiration Watto, and I applaud you on a magnificent book. Tim Nagorcka, Operations Manager & Director Horsham Hydraulics, Shed Night champion

The stuff Watto talks about will help set you free... it did for my husband, and in doing so, **has revitalised our marriage. I can't wait to buy a dozen copies to give out.** It will make an awesome Christmas present for the fellas in our lives! Really easy to read. Non-threatening, which Aussie blokes need. Watto's personality comes out on every page. It's his heart on paper, and I love it! Julie Oster, Farmer

I know who I am and Whose I am...and you will too after reading Watto's straight-to-the-point gems of wisdom— or Wattoisms as we fondly refer to them. For many years of my life I have been searching for that missing ingredient that catapults you to the next level, that good to great stuff! What I discovered in this book is that the very thing I was desperately grabbing for is already a part of who I am. **It showed me something special that has changed the way I live my life.** John Ahern, Servant/Husband/Father/Service Engineer (mining)

This book is relevant to a range of blokes from young to more mature, for those at the start, middle or towards the end of their journey of manhood. **Whether you read it from cover to cover or in small bursts, there are many words of wisdom that can be applied in your life right now.** Rhonda McKenzie, Schoolteacher

Whether you fly aeroplanes, train truck drivers, are a butcher, baker, electricity salesman or any other occupation, even unemployed, there will be tough times in your life. They could be related to alcoholism, depression, money, sex, marital problems, the list goes on. They create 'rocks' in your heart. **Pick up Watto's book, have a read and let change begin. Watto is a 'heart' man and tells it as it is. He wants you to be the real-deal.** Not only will healing commence, but you will become a much better bloke (champion) in all aspects of your life, and yes! I do speak from personal experience. Timothy Nagel, Airline Pilot

EVERY BLOKE'S A CHAMPION... EVEN YOU!

'shed happens'

Men learn from men,
as iron sharpens iron.
Proverbs 27:17

G'day mate...

www.shednight.com

Ten years ago I helped kick off Shed Nights for blokes – not the Sheds where men work with their hands but a different type of Shed that goes like this...

It starts off with a ripper burger at 6:30pm in a safe non-judgemental place where men can hear real-deep gut issues – good, bad, happy or sad – through two or three blokes being interviewed up front. It's held on the first Monday of each month and up to 200 blokes from all walks of life enjoy being together.

Shed Happens as blokes encourage each other as they do the journey of life together. They are more than happy to tell it as it is from the heart, so that others can be helped. Shed is a place where blokes are champions for who they are – not for what they are or what they have. No-one is allowed to preach, but only to tell their own story.

I go to many different places in Australia helping blokes get their Sheds happening. So that's why my book contains references to Shed and the freedom that blokes experience in their emotions, heads, souls and spirits, through being in a safe place to spill their guts and become the real-deal.

Hope you enjoy Shed on the **shednight.com** website

Watto

Foreword

I often wonder how other people see Ian. To me, he is my father, but he is also my hero, encourager, leveller, advisor and yardstick on life. I admire his courage, passion, willingness to help and encourage others and ability to challenge and push people out of their comfort zone.

The book you are about to read is genuinely Ian Watson. It is written as Ian would say it and to principles by which he lives his life. It is a privilege to have Ian as my father.

He has not left any stone unturned in his responsibility to be a good father to me and my two brothers and our families. He is not afraid to show his emotions and struggles. I know that I count on him to put himself on the line for me. It is easy for me to know my Father in Heaven by the example that my earthly father provides.

I believe that God gave my father a sledge-hammer to open men's hearts so that they can be healed and blessed. He can also make you feel like you are getting a half time footy talk and leaves you wanting to run through the dressing room wall to get into the game of life. I hope that you enjoy this book and receive all the above benefits and more.

Haydn Watson

CONTENTS

Foreword	viii
I've never seen a bloke go backwards with encouragement	1
1. Champions blast off from turbocharged words!	4
2. Champions dream dreams	21
3. Champions conquer hatred, bitterness, resentment and unforgiveness	41
4. Champions listen	57
5. Champions emerge from knowing about the Bloke Upstairs to knowing him	73
6. Champions honour their father and mother, so that 'all goes well'	96
7. Champions grow into trust	111
8. Champions handle anger	126
9. Champions know and apply tough/directional love and gentle/nurture love when needed	142
10. Champions grow to know that love gives life and lust takes life	159
11. Champions can give it and receive it	174
12. Hearts are trumps	191
Champions become the real-deal bloke for all occasions	215

Thanks!

To my champion wife Margaret for typing my book just the way it came out of my heart.

To our three champion sons, Haydn, Brendan and Luke – for bringing joy into our lives.

To my champion editor Belinda Pollard who had to think like 'Watto'.

To all the champions in my life and in my Shed.

To the Champion of champions for breathing life into me.

Watto

I've never seen a bloke go backwards with encouragement

This book happened after I spoke at a men's Shed Night in Dubbo NSW, and a B-double truckie came up to me. He said, 'Hey Watto, you said something worth remembering: I've never seen a bloke go backwards with encouragement.'

That's one of my favourite sayings, because I've discovered that encouragement is one of the main keys to champion living. As an office worker, a soldier for two years, an AFL footy coach, a truck driver, and a truck driving instructor, I've enjoyed a lifetime of helping and encouraging men old and young in footy, driving, doing business, and just plain old Doing Life.

Life can be a battle and no-one misses out on the hard parts. They just have different names and times. But if the hard parts don't kill you, I reckon it's gotta be good for you eventually. And encouragement can make all the difference.

Life is my passion. I like to live it, not look at it. I've had a great life and enjoyed every part of my manhood – the good, the bad, the happy, the sad. I've been in the trenches with fellow blokes and I've seen the things that smash men's hearts and the things that turbocharge them into the champion team.

That Dubbo truckie's comment got me thinking that if I put down on paper some of the gems I've been given on the journey of my life, they could help many more blokes enjoy being the real-deal, living as the men they were created to be.

My wish is for this to be one of those books that you can pick up any time or place. You can read a little or a lot and extract an absolute diamond each time. After you cruise through my little book, I hope it will help you sort out any bumps or lumps on your journey. Then you can be free to be the real-deal bloke you were created to be, and attack and enjoy the rest of your life.

The Aussie Bloke is a great bloke. But he's generally shy and a one-on-one bloke when it gets down to the Real Deep Guts issues. He'll spill it if he's in a safe non-judgemental place, to get freedom in his own life, and to help someone else avoid hitting the wall.

My business motto that's painted on the side of all my trucks is: '**Come and let me treat you like a champion**'. And it works! When a man is treated like the champion he is, he starts living like one. This doesn't just work in learning to drive a truck, it works in every part of life.

You don't need to be a sportsman or a genius or wealthy enough to own a helicopter to be a champion bloke. **You are a champion!** Let me show you how to more-become the real-deal champion you were created to be.

Mate, this is my heart-to-heart to you. Come on the journey with me and we'll have a red-hot crack at the champion way of real-deal living.

The billy's always boiling!
Love ya guts

Watto

1. Champions blast off from turbocharged words!

TO GET YOU STARTED

Mate, are you hearing a special turbocharged word deep down in your heart that's just for you?

Or have you numbed yourself not to go there because you missed out in the past? That can happen to a bloke, but you don't have to stay 'deaf' to these special words.

I'm going to show you how to take that turbocharged word and launch off into the champion team.
This book is my turbocharged word to **you**!

Turbocharged words that launch champions

One day, 2 of my truckie mates happened to be having haircuts at my 'barber shop' which was under our house in the laundry. Big Jonesy was one of them, and I thought the world of him. He was 10 years older and wiser than I was, and **his words meant plenty to me.**

1. CHAMPIONS BLAST OFF FROM TURBOCHARGED WORDS

I told these 2 mates that I was planning to leave the security of my office job and buy a truck. They both burst out laughing. Jonesy said, '**Watto, you're a bloody idiot. Leave that bludgy job?**' They were just teasing me, the way blokes do. I tried not to show it but my pride and ego were smashed.

It didn't stay that way, though. Jonesy must have somehow seen that this was important to me. **His face changed and he looked me in the eye and said, 'Watto, you'll never look back.'** His words came from the bottom of his big heart and I felt it smack bang in the middle of my heart. Jonesy had affirmed me. His words meant: '**You're OK, and you'll be good at it!**' It was a turbocharged word just for me.

When someone you love, admire and respect empowers you, you are ready to launch to the moon. It can put a whole new life and purpose into you.

> **Have you had a word like this?**
> **Perhaps you have but you might have missed it?**
> **Let's help you be ready for the next turbocharged word coming your way.**

Words that turn out to be winners

So, how do you know what to listen for? Sometimes a turbocharged word from a mate can lead you to do unexpected things, with great results! And that mate might not even realise it's a turbocharged word. But if you listen and keep yourself open, you never know what you might hear.

The reason I was doing haircuts for truckies in my laundry that day goes right back to when I was conscripted to do my 2 years' compulsory army service in the 60s during the Vietnam War. **One of my mates gave me a turbocharged word that stuck and proved a winner for me in a lot more ways than he or I imagined.**

He went to basic training in the intake before me. When I asked if he had any tips for me, he said, '**Yeah, one bloke in the whole joint was the platoon barber and all he did was mow the hair off. Didn't even have to be good at it. My tip is: be the platoon barber.**'

I thought, *I can do that.*

So I went out and bought a set of hairdresser's clippers and practised on my father and father-in-law to be. Their haircuts were rough as guts, but I was just getting into it.

After about 10 haircuts, I took off for the army base at Singleton NSW. On my first parade, the sergeant called out, 'Have we a barber in the platoon?' I bravely raised my hand, and then realised that I was the only one with my hand up.

He said, '**Recruit Watson, you will be the official platoon barber.**'

From that turbocharged word from my mate, my business life began. 'Watson, you will use room 12D as your barber shop. Keep it clean. You will charge $2, and of that, 50c will go towards the platoon booze-up at the end of training.'

As the army was only interested in the hair that wasn't under your hat, most of my haircuts were the 'number one' all over. I couldn't go wrong – just cut it off.

At the end of my 12 weeks at Singleton, the haircuts paid for my flight home. Later when I was transferred to Victoria Barracks in Brisbane, I cut the hair of the high-ranking officers, and some of them taught me valuable things about business and leadership. What a good word from my mate who noticed this opportunity!

I continued to give haircuts for many years after that. They were mostly freebies. One of my customers had only one ear. Even though this was not actually as a result of my work, the standard joke was that his haircut was a Watto Special. Come down the shed one day and I'll give you a Watto Special too!

So, my business life began from a turbocharged word from a mate.

Winning words that stick

We blokes all need the affirming words of another man, and never stop needing it, no matter how old. We are always following some bloke we admire and someone is following us, even though we may not realise it. I never forgot Jonesy's word that I'd be a good truck driver, and I never looked back. Thanks, Big Jonesy. The affirming word sticks!

> Pass on the turbocharged affirming word
> to those you know need to hear it,
> and see them fly.
> But don't patronise
> otherwise they will not hear it.
> Blokes like you to call it as it is
> and straight down the line – no bull.

The words of a father

We boys and men need that turbocharged encouraging and empowering word from our fathers, or at least another respected male.

My mother powerfully affirmed me, but my Dad used the opposite tack. He used to say, 'You're a show-off. Stop skiting.' My personality is definitely larger than life and yes, I do have plenty to say. I have an opinion and a solution to all problems. I was and still am super-confident to some, a little arrogant, seen to be 'up yourself', a lair.

Later in life, my relationship with Dad improved. We got it together. He came to the footy with me and we went to the trotting together. I now know he loved me and wanted the best for me.

But in my youth, **Dad kept me down with words** – you know what I mean? I think it was his way of making me humble, but instead of thinking about it and learning from it, I was discouraged by those words. They hurt my heart deep inside. I wanted him to tell me how good I was.

Maybe he wanted me to be more determined as a result of his strategy. Well, it worked eventually. I didn't stay down forever.

> **If you've been talked down by your father, how did you react to it? Did you use it as a springboard to get up and go, or did you crumble? Now's the time to get up!**

'Accidental' turbocharged words

My grandmother lived into her nineties, a powerful old matriarch and maverick who wore tangerine socks!

One day she pushed the wrong number on her speed dial and got my phone by mistake. 'Oh darling,' she said, 'I thought I was talking to Dorothy. You're a wonderful boy. I just want you to know that I pray for you every day. God bless you Ian.' And she put the phone down.

I ran into the bedroom and jumped on the bed and cried like a little boy. Yes, I'm a big sook and that's the way I react when I feel really emotional all of a sudden! The part deep inside of me was so joyful, because it hit me: *Here's my dear grandmother, this old lady with impaired vision who a lot of people probably think is a bit eccentric, and she prays for every family member by name every day. No wonder I've got such a fantastic life.* She called a wrong number by accident, **but her words turbocharged my day.**

Steer clear of killing words

Discouraging words can kill. Sure, you might not drop dead on the spot, but they kill you on the inside. Your heart and your dreams and your courage die a little bit when someone says you're no good.

> **Don't take them into your heart.
> Refuse them at your head level.
> If needed, check out with a trusted bloke,
> to see if you need to deal further
> with any hard, discouraging words.**

One way to deflect a killing word can be to think about a turbocharged word you've received another time. Instead of letting it smash your heart, remind yourself of a positive thing that someone else has said about you. This can also help en**courage** you when you are facing a challenge like asking a girl on a date or asking the boss for a raise! It can help make you stronger against the possible killing word that may come.

Sadly, some people say killing words to make themselves feel superior. **Let all killing words aimed at you go through to the keeper.** Receive empowering words and encouragement.

And try not to be a person who gives killing words. Think before you speak. Are you about to kill someone's dream or break their heart?

Learn how to welcome turbocharged words

When you receive a complimentary empowering turbocharged word, just say thank you. Believe it and accept it. Get on with it.

Don't go on with, 'Aw, you don't mean that, you're just saying that. I'm not really that good.' That's not champion. Someone wants to empower you and you're restricting it.

Far too many blokes are held back because when someone offers a compliment or a good word they reject it or fob it off. They think they're trying to be humble. We Aussie blokes can even get to the hating-ourselves point, which is so cruel.

Champions blast off from turbocharged words!

> Sadly, in our culture there can be an expectancy
> not to see yourself too highly,
> not to accept
> that someone sees the champion in you,
> and hold back from being yourself.

Champion, take the good and positive turbocharged word when offered. It can blast you off into a new and exciting life and you can see, feel and experience the 'real-deal you' emerging.

Back in my AFL days at Sandgate Hawks Footy Club in Brisbane, I recall Don Smith winning the Best and Fairest footballer trophy year after year. His speech on receiving the trophy was: 'Thank you, and thank you to my team-mates.' He didn't have to say any more. He didn't go on with all the predictable excuses for being the best, but he didn't get carried away with his own importance either. He was a humble champion. **He knew he was the best player and accepted the fair word.**

Champion, when someone gives you a good word – relax, enjoy, say thank you. No need to say more.

Learn how to give encouraging turbocharged words

'Do not withhold good from those who deserve it, when it is in your power to act' (Proverbs 3:27). That little gem is from my favourite book, the Bible, which has so much practical advice for blokes that I call it the *Work Manual for the Champion*

Life. (Try to get a chance to read it sometime – you might be surprised how good it is, like I was!)

Don't hold back with your turbocharged word to those who deserve it. When you have the power to encourage someone else, **say what's in your heart. Just speak out honestly and watch them fly!**

If you feel strange and you don't know how to do this, try practising a turbocharged warm-and-fuzzy word on a baby if there's one nearby. Little babies bring something amazing out of a bloke, we let the guard down.

Come on, let go, try it, it won't hurt you. The *Work Manual* says some more about this: 'If we can encourage others, we should encourage them' (Romans 12:8) and 'We should keep on encouraging each other to be thoughtful and to do helpful things' (Hebrews 10:25).

Have the courage to just gently let the word come out, and then don't spend the next week justifying what you said. If it's positive and it's come from the heart, just let it be.

People don't die from over-praise or over-encouragement. I've never seen a bloke go backwards with encouragement!

Say what you mean and mean what you say

A man whose words had a big impact on my life was Andrew Ireland, the Collingwood AFL player who became CEO of AFL in

Queensland. Later he was CEO of the Brisbane Lions and now the CEO of the Sydney Swans. He empowered me by his words of encouragement in my coaching for 2 years, and then for 8 years as team manager of the Under 17 AFL Queensland team.

He took me from the local club mentality to the top level of the AFL. I respected him and knew he meant what he said. It brought out the real me. We moulded a team of champions over that period of my life, enjoying so many champion moments.

Andrew quietly and powerfully gave me the nod. We developed trust over time to know that we meant what we said and each other's words could be counted on. **Say what you mean and mean what you say!**

What about a hard word?

A young player who came into one of our squads was known as Mad Dog. He lived and acted this name that was imposed on him, doing what everyone expected him to do. Up to that stage of his life he knew no other way. He offended all the other players with his mad-dog attitude and lifestyle.

We wanted him in the team because he could play. We needed the hard type of player he was.

But when it came time to make our final selection, we knew we couldn't include him because of the way the other players felt about him. His presence would have totally disrupted the team flow and culture.

So I was given the task of a one-on-one talk with Mad Dog to explain the situation. If he could accept his true identity in who he was as Tim, his real name – the tough, straight at the ball, no beg pardons player who could play his part in the team on and off the field – then he could be welcomed into the team.

He chose to turn 180 degrees from Mad Dog to Tim.

Before that, Tim hadn't really heard an encouraging or empowering word spoken to him from a respected fellow male, so he just did same-old-same-old. But at that moment he knew in his heart that we officials meant what we said and could see the champion in him. He listened to the call to challenge his identity. **He wanted to be accepted, and chose to be a new man.**

We gathered the other squad members together at our team meeting and told them that we had let go the player called Mad Dog, and replaced him with a new and exciting hard-player called Tim. I took him round the room, and one-on-one, eye-to-eye, introduced the new player. There were tears of excitement as a young champion bloke emerged. Tim went on to be the best team man of the carnival.

He never looked back. **He was empowered by turbocharged words deep down in his heart.** It was a complete turnaround.

This is for you too. Don't hold back from becoming the real-deal champion you were created to be. Accept the empowering turbocharged words you're given, to be the real-deal. You can't be better than that!

We don't always know if or how our turbocharged words work

Sometimes empowering words backfire… or do they?

I spoke encouragement to a class of boys at a school in the northern suburbs of Brisbane 20 years ago. Just recently I was reminded by the teacher who was there that day that I had given away a bloke's book: *You can make a difference* by Tony Campolo.

Before the talk I told the boys I had asked the Bloke Upstairs to show me the person I was to give the book to.

At the end of the talk, I stood like a stunned mullet thinking, *God, who is he? Who do you want me to give the book to?* I looked around the room in desperation. Nothing. Blank. That sorts out your ego! It was a good lesson for me not to 'play God' and demand magic signs.

So I just handed it to a young bloke, and that was that. I thought it was a disaster.

However, 20 years later I've discovered how that young man at that stage of his life was not in the best of places. **He read the book, took it into his heart, and powered on and up into a champion place.** Today he is the principal of a large school. God turned what I thought was my 'failure' into a turbocharged word for that young man. How God made it happen is his business, not mine!

Encourage another bloke who doesn't think he's good enough

Over the past 4 years through Shed Happens, I've been privileged to encourage many men about manhood. But there have been times where I've needed encouragement to keep on going myself.

Two highly respected blokes gave me turbocharged empowering words when I needed them.

I could have been intimidated about sharing speaking duties at a camp with a highly qualified teacher. **The first of these encouraging men said, 'Just be yourself, Watto.'**

The other encourager said to me before another event, **'Don't change anything. Just continue to be and speak out how God made you. That's why men can listen to you, because it's real and they respect you.'**

Both these men have been my mentors at different times and I respect them very much. What they said counted.

> What about you?
> Are you hearing that special word
> deep down in your heart
> that's just for you?
> Or have you numbed yourself not to go there,
> and just half-hear it in your head?

There are many, many of these stories of blokes emerging out of the crap of the world to become champions. From time to time, someone in your life will give you a genuine turbocharged word. **Hear it, and take it in. You are OK.**

The take-home message

We need to learn how to give the turbocharged word. But it must come from our hearts as we speak it into the other person's heart.

You reap what you sow. So says the *Work Manual* (Galatians 6:7 NIV). If you want to see a tree grow, you've got to plant the right seed. If I want my business to be successful, I've got to get in and do the hard yards. I can't just sit back. If I expect to sit down and wait for someone to give me money or success, why should they? But if I get out and actually **give and plant and serve, it comes back in bucket loads.**

It's the same with words: you reap what you sow.

If you want to dump crap on someone, just get ready, because it's going to come back to you in bucket loads.

Remember the old saying: do unto others as you would have them do unto you? It works for words too. Say unto others what you would have them say unto you!

The more you plant the more you harvest, and you'll be well on the way to becoming the real-deal champion you were created to be. Plant good and encouraging turbocharged words into people and you will reap good and encouraging words that will empower you for your day-to-day living.

> ## TO REMEMBER...
>
> All blokes need an affirming, turbocharged word.
>
> If you get an empowering turbocharged word, just say thank you, and enjoy!
>
> A hard word can give life if it comes from the heart.
>
> A hard word from the head can kill a bloke's dreams.
>
> Blokes don't die from over-praise or encouraging words.
>
> I've never seen a bloke go backwards with a turbocharged word of encouragement.

BONUS:

Fellas, a few little gems from the *Work Manual*. There is so much wisdom in there about the power of words – both turbocharged words and killing words. Just think about each one for a bit, and see if it encourages you to use your words to encourage.

> **Kind words are good medicine**, but deceitful words can really hurt. (Proverbs 15:4)

> Losing your temper is foolish; **ignoring an insult is smart**. An honest person tells the truth in court, but a dishonest person tells nothing but lies. **Sharp words cut**

like a sword, but words of wisdom heal. **Truth will last forever; lies are soon found out.** (Proverbs 12:16-20)

You can persuade others if you are wise and speak sensibly. **Kind words are like honey— they cheer you up and make you feel strong.** (Proverbs 16:23-24)

And finally, a good thing to say every day...

Help me to guard my words whenever I say something. (Psalm 141:3)

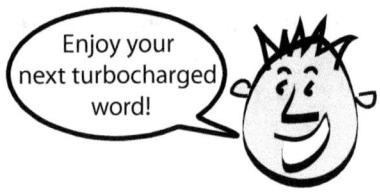

2. Champions dream dreams

> **TO GET YOU STARTED**
>
> Have you got a dream right this moment?
> How's it coming along?
>
> Are you OK to dream dreams,
> or have you put the shutters up because you can't see that your dream will ever happen?
> Have you had dreams
> that don't seem to have amounted to anything?
> Have you been smashed by dream-takers?
>
> Let's get to the dreams that are deep within us all, and nurture them into life.

Dreams come from a deep, deep place inside who we are, from a turbocharged part of our being. **They are much more than just head-thoughts.**

Dreams take you into a new place. Even the word sounds good! Say it aloud, champion: 'Dream…'

A dream is what happens when you have the courage to let go and let that little inner voice come out of you. It says: *I want to 'climb the mountain', I want to make a difference.*

Most of the time we never get to that deep place of dreams, because we're too consumed by 'stuff': work, the mortgage, trying to get up the ladder, never really having enough money to do what we want. We get pulled down by 'If only...' and 'I should have...'.

But there's still that something deep within men. **We want the challenge, we want the adventure, we want to achieve, we want to provide, we want to solve problems.**

The difference a dream makes

Have you ever been to another country where the pollution is so bad that the sky is always grey? The sky and the countryside and the buildings and even the people look grey. People who live there don't know what it's like to have a clear blue sky – the brightness and the light and the colours. They don't know there's anything else to see!

That's what it's like living without a dream. You live in dullness, and that's where the anxieties and depressions are. But there's more to life than that.

When we start to see the blue sky and get into the light, our dreams come out and ignite us. Let me show you the way to the blue sky.

Have your dreams been smashed?

If a bloke's dreams have been smashed, he becomes harder inside. He doesn't dare to dream, he doesn't get courageous about things, he holds back more. He goes into 'same-old same-old' mode. He says things like, 'It's all right for you, you're young, but I've missed my time.'

When a man's dreams get smashed, it's like a sponge that used to be full of water but has slowly dried out. **The sponge is still there, but it needs life. Give it life! Give it water!** It's not dead yet.

As a boy, I dreamed of being a schoolteacher. I wanted to teach physical education (PE). I loved sport and I was a natural leader. But I didn't win a scholarship to go to teacher's college, and **my father couldn't afford to pay for me to study. My dreams were smashed. I was dulled and disappointed and dejected.** I thought, *That's the end of it.*

As I sat at my desk in my pencil-pushing job for the next 22 years, I didn't even give it my best shot. I felt trapped. Blokes looking in from the outside saw my great superannuation and my flexitime and envied my security. But it didn't feel like security to me. It felt like a noose around my neck.

Well, that wasn't the end of the story, and for the past 23 years **I have been a teacher after all – a teacher of men.** I've taught blokes to drive trucks, and even better than that, I've encouraged tens of thousands of men into becoming the real-deal champions they were created to be, dreaming their own turbocharged dreams.

How's that for a smashed dream that came back to life?

Looking back, it's easy to see why it took so long for me to become a teacher.

To be a real-deal teacher of men, I needed real-deal life skills in manhood. How could I teach a man about being a man if I hadn't done the hard yards myself?

Maybe your dream is taking a long time, like mine did. But that doesn't mean it's dead. Some dreams take longer, and men need time and space.

Now I know that the Boss of all dreams, my Creator, always had me in his radar. He's got me going hard and enjoying my dream at the best time of the race – teaching and encouraging men and boys into a great life, pursuing their own dreams.

He's got you in his radar too. My dream to be a PE teacher was shattered so it could emerge as something different. Maybe your dream is being rebuilt like mine was!

Some dreams take blood, sweat and tears

I grew up loving sport and particularly Aussie Rules football. I started playing in the Deagon Under 12s on Brisbane's bayside, a feeder club to the Sandgate Hawks, and I loved every minute of it. I really charged into the team thing, and played my heart out each year for that elusive flag, right on through to the A Grade.

We always seemed to be runners up, never the winners, but then, we finally did it. Not just once, but twice. Wow! I'm excited again just thinking about it all these years later.

At that point in my life, **I thought I'd reached my sporting dream. But there was more than that**. I got to represent my state. And I got to coach the Queensland Under 17 team for 2 years in the national competition, continuing on as team manager and chairman of selectors. Wow! **My dream came true in a bigger way than I could have dreamed as a boy.**

Maybe you need to keep working at your dream too. Your thing might not be sport, but whatever it is that really switches you on, it can give you the same feeling I had when I held that premiership cup.

The feeling of being a Champion!

> Don't spend too much time bashing yourself
> because you think it ain't gonna happen.
> Just keep surging forward,
> onward and upward,
> step by step.
> Dreams happen one day at a time,
> and they take work.
> Put a bit of blood sweat and tears in behind your dream.

Some dreams change as they mature

My eldest son Haydn dreamed of playing professional AFL, but when he thought about his abilities, he decided to go to university instead and pursue an engineering career. He saw some from his age group go on to play for the Brisbane Bears, but now says he wouldn't swap his career for that.

He has accepted who he is, made choices, and gone in that new direction without regrets. **His boyhood dream matured into a different goal as he entered manhood.**

Dreams can keep you going through tough times

My identical twin nephews Peter and David are better known to many as **Peebo and Dagwood the clowns**. These two champions were born with the genetic condition cystic fibrosis (CF) which affects the lungs and digestion.

Every day of their lives has been a health battle with strict diets and countless hospital visits. **They tried to hold down full-time jobs, but their health demands made that impossible. So they adjusted their dreams and are in high demand as professional clowns.**

In 2005, they were grateful to receive lifesaving double lung transplants. Against the odds they are still living their dream at 39, giving laughter and hope to people of all ages.

They have a champion saying that I love: 'Living the dream and licking the cream'. They make the most of every part of life, and really enjoy the special bits that are like the cream on a cake, or the froth on a super-cappuccino. They make me want to reignite my own dream, and I hope their story inspires you too!

Stay close to dream-makers

While doing my office job that lasted 22 years, **I continually dreamed of getting out and being my own man.** For 22 years it only ever seemed that it was an impossibility, but the Bloke Upstairs had his plan for me. He obviously had me on a 22-year training plan to develop my man-skills ready for my 23 years of the truck driving school business. **If it's meant to be it will happen.**

In my office job, I started to dream about buying a truck, but I didn't really know anything about trucks. A mate with a backhoe suggested I buy a single-axle tipper. My other mate, Big Jonesy, was an experienced truckie. He said, 'You need an

FM 215 tipper. They're fairly new on the market. A good second-hand one is as scarce as hen's teeth. Wait till one comes up.'

I started checking the ads in the trucking section, and one day, there it was: an FM 215 tipper.

Would you believe that I went weak at the knees, and tried to avoid going to take a look at this truck that was just what I needed for my dream? I had wanted freedom from my comfortable, secure office job for years, but when the opportunity came up I had the wobbles. **Fear could have taken away my dream. Fear of the unknown. Fear of failure. Fear of what other people would think if I blew it.**

But Big Jonesy had seen the ad. So had my mate who owned a backhoe business. So I couldn't hide!

In another 'coincidence', my backhoe mate couldn't work one day because of wet weather, so he offered to take me to test-drive this truck. How could I say no? Fellas, when I got 200m from that truck yard, my heart was pounding and my knees were shaking. I was a fearful mess. My mate pulled over and said a prayer to God for me to clinch the deal on the truck. I sure needed that prayer to overcome my fear!

The asking price was $18,500. My mate advised me to offer $15,000 if they fixed a few defects first. I thought I was safe, because the seller would never accept that deal, and I wouldn't have to face the fears standing between me and my dream. But the seller did accept it!

I signed the contract, and my trucking life began, even though I was still shaking and wondering what to do next.

These two close buddies who helped me turned out to be dream-makers. They knew my dream, and they encouraged me.

Fulfilling the dream

I threw in my office job and started using the tipper to deliver soil, sand and gravel. My dream was taking shape.

The tipper just happened to have a removable steel water tank on the back, and I didn't know what to do with the tank. Big Jonesy told me to put it in a back corner of the yard and it would turn out to be a bonus one day. **Jonesy's words encouraged me to continue to dream, and to look for an opportunity to make that tank work for me.**

I saw two other local water trucks filling up at the hydrant. I found out they had domestic water delivery businesses. So I cleaned out the tank – not a real fun job jumping inside and scrubbing that out! – put a small ad in the Yellow Pages, and… nothing happened.

Then, on Boxing Day of all days, when we had friends over for a barbecue, my phone rang, and it went something like this.

Bloke on phone: 'Do you do domestic water deliveries?'

Ian: 'Well, yes.'

Bloke: 'Mate, I'm desperate for water. I've got 30 people coming and my tank's run dry. My regular water man has moved away.' He added that he usually paid $40 for a load but would give me $100 plus a bottle of champagne if I would get him out of trouble.

One hundred dollars, a bottle of champagne, and the knowledge that the regular water man had moved on, gave me the break I needed. That was Day 1 of my water business. I had a flier printed, and took my sons and a mate's family to put one in every letterbox in the water tank area. Hey presto, the dream came to life. Thirty years later, it's still going.

I could have said no to this opportunity because it was a public holiday and the guests had arrived and I was all dressed for a barbecue. **But my dream was strong. I had to take charge if I wanted to fulfil it.** Wow and pow!

Don't believe the dream-takers

Fellas, hang in there. **Don't believe jealous or scared people who can be dream-takers – get alongside dream-makers.**

Sometimes dream-takers don't even know they are stealing your dreams. When I told the blokes at work I was going to leave to buy a truck, none of them had any clue about trucks, but they all had opinions. Dream-takers put little doubts in your mind that give you the wobbles…

'Hey Watto, my neighbour's got a truck and he blew up the motor and it cost him 10 grand.'

'Gee, the price of fuel and rego's going up all the time, how will you afford it?'

'A bloke I know got taken the other day for 3 grand. Who would want to go into business?'

Don't believe everything you hear, especially from people who don't understand your dream. They may be focusing on one small detail, instead of seeing the whole picture. **Look at the big page, not just the black dot in the middle of the page.**

Some blokes may find that their woman can act like a dream-taker, opposing their dream, but a lot of the time that's because the men don't talk to the women! If you're not talking to your woman about your dream, and looking at it together with her, she might be scared. She'll feel like she has to hold on to what she's got at the moment instead of moving into something new.

If you sit down and communicate with her, you'll both have the support and confidence of each other, and you'll go forward. **The dream can recharge and reignite. Her support will turbocharge your dream!**

Champion, don't let go of your dream. The dream that was right for you will emerge somewhere along the way. Keep on keeping on, and the one who is the Giver of all dreams will determine your destiny for you.

You might feel like you're in prison because of where you are at in life, like I did in that office job. You can spend your life looking at the 'bars' of your 'prison', or you can look out your window at those beautiful stars the Big Fella's put in the sky.

Dream-takers will try to make you focus on the bars, but it's your choice. Look up and out. **See the stars, not the bars.**

Tell dream-makers your dream

It's OK to dream your dreams – and don't be shy. Tell others about it. Blokes can do it!

So many blokes are dealing with depression and anxiety and loneliness, because they're isolated from other blokes. When men get together for the right reasons in a good safe place, something happens that's just amazing. It energises and it sticks, and it helps you to ignite your dream.

Through Shed Happens, I've seen thousands of men being transformed by being able to talk out the gut issues with other blokes. Every week around Australia, men meet in sheds and encourage each other (you can find one near you at shednight.com). It's a safe, non-judgemental place. They get a new life and identity in who they are and what they do, and they fly into champion living. They can once again dream healthy dreams.

At shed groups, I see the 'great Aussie bloke' enjoying and attacking life, and becoming more real in who he was created to be.

As men start to get their dreams back, I see excitement and energy coming out of them. It's a joy that comes from deep within. A lot of men have been judged or ignored or brushed off. When you spend the time to ask them how their heart's going and they know they're in a safe place, great things can happen. Dreams begin to live.

My dream

I have a dream to see a Big Shed Night with 50,000 champion blokes in each of the big footy stadiums around Australia. They'll rub shoulders with fellow champions, tell joyful stories, and build and learn from each other.

It's a bit scary to speak out this dream of mine, because I might get mud on my face. It's a huge dream and many people might say it is impossible.

But then, when I do speak about it, other men around me take the dream onwards.

This is how a dream happens. I just said, 'We'll fill Suncorp Stadium in Brisbane one night.' A couple of my young guns, intelligent young men, said, 'Watto, why stop at Suncorp Stadium? What about the other blokes in the rest of Australia? Why don't we have a simulcast, all over Australia.' Wow!

I'm 66. When is this dream going to come to life? It might be next year, or when I'm 86, or it might be my grandson standing there with 50,000 blokes saying, **'This was my Pop's dream.'**

Aussie blokes are firing up in these little 'bushfires' in sheds all around the country. One day, someone's going to say, 'Let's all get together!' and my dream will happen.

Men with changed and free hearts can change Australia. If you want to see good change at the top, you've got to get a revolution at the bottom. **When these men all rise up together, the whole nation will change. Men will be more secure in who they are, knowing they are the real-deal and knowing they are OK.**

The real-deal dream

Every bloke's dream is different, so what is the real-deal dream for you? If you don't know what it is, how do you find it?

We've been conditioned to live life in our heads, and think things must all add up logically and come to a sensible conclusion. But dreams don't come from the head. They come from the heart.

When you are courageous to go deep, deep into your heart, and let the dreams in your heart come out, your head and your heart combine into a freshness, a newness, an excitement. Then dreams can happen.

To unearth the dreams within you, you might have to dare to go back to how you felt when you were a little boy. It can be scary, but hang in there, it's worth it.

I reckon the best way to tap into your dreams is to talk to the Bloke Upstairs about it. But if you're not at a stage where you want to do that, then this is what I suggest. Get away on your own, away from all the 'stuff' of jobs and responsibilities and mortgages, and don't take your mobile phone.

You might go to a beach or to the bush. Just truly get away where there's nothing to take your mind off who you are. Let your mind relax and go with it. Write down any hopes and ideas that come out of who you are. Dare to dream.

These days, most of us don't spend enough time sitting still and having a bit of a think. When I'm on my own now, I try to be quiet, and I don't often turn on the TV. I don't even turn on the radio when I'm alone in my car; I use that for thinking time. **Sometimes we think we need to be entertained and we're not game to give ourselves the time or silence to dream.**

Training for dreams

Like many fathers, I always wanted my boys to have the university degree I never had. I knew this motto from the *Work Manual*: 'Train up a child in the way he should go and when he is old he will not depart from it' (Proverbs 22:6 NKJV). It's a good motto, isn't it?

From a young age my boys knew that their education journey would include primary school, high school and university. But the Bloke Upstairs showed me that 'education' and 'training a child in the way he should go' is much more than school or TAFE or a Cert III or university. Sometimes the university of hard knocks can be the most handy training tool.

It ain't all about reading, writing and 'rithmetic. It's about what you learn from life's challenges. It's about discovering who you are and where you want to go.

I could tell you lots of stories about my 3 son's journeys and how they kept plugging away at their dreams. Some of their dreams took longer than we expected. Some of their dreams changed over time and ended up as goals. They learned a lot of things that aren't taught at university, about real-life people skills and appreciating your fellow man, by doing life with many different people as they grew into young men.

Their Creator's plan was bigger than any of my expectations. I am so proud of them.

The Creator's plan is bigger than your expectations too. This book is to encourage you on the journey to where you want to go – your real-deal dream. Whether you go to university or TAFE or not, it doesn't matter. And let's look for opportunities to become a dream-maker for someone else.

There's still time for a bloke to mature, even at 33 or 35. **We need to stop rushing our young men, and just encourage them in their future.** If we keep alongside them we can help their dreams to emerge.

I've grown to become a big fan of a bloke named Jesus as I've heard more about him. He was a carpenter, a chippie, who trained up for the first 30 years of his life to get ready to teach and challenge people for the next 3 years. He hit the mark for us all at 33 when he died to save the world. He wasn't late, he was right on time.

Could that mean something for each of us blokes? **We're never too old to learn and change, so keep on dreaming your dream.**

Dreams and the Big Fella

My sons and grandsons regularly hear from me that they are champions just because they are who they are, and they are good enough the way they are. I encourage them to remember Whose they are. **They and their dreams belong to their Creator.**

You might still be making up your mind whether you think God is for real or not. That's OK. It took me a long time. I don't go trying to tell everyone to do this or think that. **No-one proves God to anyone.**

I've been through the blood, sweat and tears of life, just like everybody else. I called out and asked him, 'Show me in my life. I need to know that you're for real!'

If you want to know whether God's for real or not, **ask him to show you in your own life whether he's for real or whether he's a fairytale.** Just keep asking him until he shows you.

You can have dreams without knowing the Big Fella. You can get encouraged by dream-makers, and your life will show more of the real-deal champion bloke inside you.

But I've discovered that God is the ultimate Dream-Maker. With his help, I am gradually becoming everything I can be.

The most turbocharged dreams of my life have come from discovering my Creator's plans for me, step by step. **His dreams for me are bigger than the ones I could dream for myself!**

The take-home message

Make a dream part of your life today. You're never too old to dream. It's very healthy.

You may never have been encouraged to dream, or you may have had your young dreams squashed.

> **Don't give up your dream! Boys are always a work in progress.**
> **Keep yourself in good company of good men and be accountable.**
> **Don't lower the bar.**
> **Keep your dream.**
> **Don't believe the dream-takers.**
> **Get with the dream-makers.**

Champion, don't panic if it takes a little longer. Just keep plugging on towards the goal. 'Inch by inch is a cinch, yard by yard is too hard.'

You can do it! Get in the champion's company. Hang on and don't let go.

The Bloke Upstairs gives you the dream, the hope to hold onto it, and the opportunity to fulfil it. I needed 22 years of life skills before I was right for my 'teaching men' role – not the original schoolteacher dream, but a life teacher. It's been fantastic.

Everyone is different and we should never lose our dreams even if they look far off.

Don't forget, **the hardest part is to start.** The bike won't move unless you push the pedal down and keep it moving.

Speak your dream out of your heart. Join a local shed group so other blokes can encourage you. Remember, you'll find a list of shed groups at shednight.com. If there's currently no shed meeting near where you live, you can talk to other blokes on the website. Speak to someone who cares about you. Tell them your dream. **Write it down.**

What's your dream? Let it come out. What are you doing about it?

Dream on. **You can do it.**

TO REMEMBER

Dream your dreams.

Your dreams can happen.

Get dream-makers around you and away you can go.

Never lose your openness to dream a dream.

BONUS:

A few more inspiring dream words from the *Work Manual* for blokes who know Whose they are:

'For I know the plans I have for you,' declares the Lord, 'plans to prosper you and not to harm you, **plans to give you hope and a future.** Then you will call on me and come and pray to me, and I will listen to you. **You will seek me**

and find me when you seek me with all your heart.' (Jeremiah 29:11-13 NIV)

You are the one who put me together inside my mother's body, and **I praise you because of the wonderful way you created me**. Everything you do is marvellous! Of this I have no doubt. Nothing about me is hidden from you! I was secretly woven together deep in the earth below, but with your own eyes you saw my body being formed. **Even before I was born, you had written in your book everything I would do.** (Psalm 139:13-16)

3. Champions conquer hatred, bitterness, resentment and unforgiveness

> **TO GET YOU STARTED**
>
> Do you feel like fresh fruit out of season,
> all sour and you don't know why?
> Have you shut down in your relationships?
> Do people have to watch their p's and q's
> and keep their guard up not to offend you?
> Are your jokes sarcastic?
>
> When was the last time you let go with a big belly laugh?
>
> Mate, we can sort this one out together – it's winnable!

Give yourself a break

Fellas, sometimes bad things happen. When they do, it's OK to have a pity party or to feel sorry for yourself for a time.

Just get on your own for a little 'veggie' time or a good long shower. Don't be too hard on yourself if you feel bad. It might last for a few days, but you don't have to buckle under it.

Don't isolate yourself for too long, though. A pity party that goes on forever won't help you be the real-deal champion you were created to be. **You can temporarily 'veggie' out, chill out – but don't bail out permanently!**

How you sort it out from here is what gets you free inside. Then the real you can emerge so you can be who you are – a champion.

Don't ignore it and think it will go away

Bitterness, hatred, resentment and unforgiveness goes down deep, and comes back to bite every so often when someone or something pushes your button.

Bitterness is like a pimple that grows into a boil. You can put a dressing over a pimple and try to forget about it, but one day the boil comes to a head and has to erupt. When the junk comes out, the healing can begin. It's the same for us blokes. We have to get the poison out of our systems before we can heal.

Resentment is like nutgrass. It you don't get to the root of the bitterness, get the weed-killer out and give the problem a good squirt, it will grow back. You've gotta go deep to get to the guts of the problem.

Forgive and forget?

Too often today we hear, '**I can never forgive that so-and-so.** He's out of my mind for the rest of my life.' Mate, that's definitely not the healthiest course of action, and it doesn't work anyway. You won't forget the pain that was deep and long, even if you think you have. Somewhere, someday it will raise its ugly head and bite big-time.

We need to nail the bitterness once and for all so we can become more real in who we were created to be.

One of my mates is a counsellor now living in Australia who was forced off his land in Zimbabwe, and he experienced terrible things – people gunned down right in front of their loved ones and other horrors. His own family has suffered tragedies that most of us can't imagine in nice, safe Australia. He has had a lot of learning and practising at forgiveness.

He says **forgiveness of the really big ones mostly needs to happen layer by layer by layer.** The operation can take time.

So don't panic if you can't just click your fingers and forgive in one hit. Hang in there and know that step by painful step you can be free from this. You may lose the occasional battle but you don't need to lose the war.

You can do it! Open up and let it out.

We need to give up the need to get even. That's forgiveness.

We need to let go and experience freedom as a champion and let the Big Fella take care of it.

Even if you don't want to believe in God, you can have a red-hot crack at forgiving someone. Find someone you can trust to help you let go, layer by painful layer. Sometimes it will take a long time.

There will be some things from the past that you can't sort out. Maybe the person is dead, or they don't want to sort it out with you, or it wasn't even their fault, it just happened. Hanging onto those kind of hurts, thinking about them again and again, is as much use as trying to saw sawdust; it just uses up energy and doesn't achieve anything. **You can't saw sawdust – you've got to let some things go.**

What resentment did to me and my family

I know what I'm talking about with hatred and bitterness.

As I said before, **my mum died when I was 15.** I found her dead on the floor, killed by an electrical fault in the washing machine. Seven years later, **my younger sister Rhonda collapsed and died at 17** from an undiagnosed heart defect. I got a double whammy of stress and trauma from grief. I was an emotional mess.

My widowed father worked very hard to provide for his 4 children. My eldest sister was 17 when my mother died, and she did the best she could at mothering us, but it's not the same.

We needed a mother. The woman who lived up the road had lost her husband to illness and she had 2 children. Two years after Mum died, she and Dad thought, 'Maybe this can work.' My dad married her and we all had family again – 2 parents and 6 children.

Everything seemed OK on the surface, but **the stuff that built up on the inside was never considered or discussed.** I was expected to get over it and get on with it. **But my pain was too deep. I needed big healing that I didn't get for many years.** At 17, life didn't look that rosy for me. I had a smashed and mixed-up heart.

Woe is me!

When Dad married his new wife, I felt like he was abandoning us. I didn't even know how to see his side of the situation.

I over-reacted big-time towards him, his new wife and her 2 children. **I unknowingly built up bitterness and resentment inside towards them all.**

One night, I actually tried to talk Dad out of marrying her. I told him that my 3 sisters and I would get on OK on our own. I couldn't hear any part of his needs. When I look back now I can see that he gave me the honour of letting me talk. **He listened to me all night until I'd talked myself dry. He didn't fob me off.**

That's a lesson to me. If your son or someone else wants to have a 'bitch' about something, don't try to justify your actions, let them speak it out. Find out what's going on.

Dad kept working his guts out, doing his best to provide. He continued his strong directional love to me to grow up and toughen up! I wanted and needed the other love and nurture – fluffy and soft. I believed that no-one cared about poor me.

I had a big chip on my shoulder but I didn't know it. I went around getting other people to tell me how wonderful I was and how life was so unfair to me.

I built up resentment and bitterness towards my father who gave it his all doing his best, but I didn't understand what he was trying to do for his children at the time.

My stepmother had a hard job. I wanted nothing less than my mother. I made judgement after judgement based on my grief and my broken heart. I saw her as unfair, giving the best to her two children. I built up bitterness and jealousy towards her.

I had stuff all built up inside and didn't know what to do with it. She was on the receiving end of lots of my frustrations. **I didn't know it but I kept her away.** I would have been an obnoxious little creep! I had plenty of reasons to be like that because I was in deep pain and I didn't know what to do about it.

Getting to the guts of it

I didn't deserve my mother's death, nor my father marrying again. I didn't deserve having to share my father with others and getting sent to the back of the queue (as it seemed to me).

When I look back I didn't have anyone to talk man-to-boy with. I didn't hit it off with Dad at that time in my young life. I felt like he was always busy working, angry and worried about money. But my 2 sisters saw him as the opposite of this, so you can see how mixed-up I was. I never even considered that the girls might have thought he was the most wonderful father in town.

I could justify all my 'woe is me' stuff to myself. That's where I would still be if it hadn't been for the freedom from coming to know who I am and Whose I am.

> When I got rid of my garbage
> and stopped trying to build up points of resentment and bitterness,
> I allowed my father's wife to change towards me.
> I had been keeping her away.

Now that I'm the real-deal Watto, I can finally love her. She's 87 and I know she loves me. She gives me kisses when I visit. I've been healed of the bitterness. I've gone from resenting her to loving her.

I had built up rocks around my heart so no-one could get in. The *Work Manual* says: 'I will give you a new heart and put a new spirit in you; I will remove from you your heart of stone and give you a heart of flesh' (Ezekiel 36:26 NIV). And that's what happened for me.

> I had to get over
>   my bitterness and resentment
>   for my whole family to change.

Basic biology

We are what we eat, so we'd best eat healthy. It's the same with thoughts. If we fill our heads with bitter thoughts, they will affect what comes out of us. Unforgiveness eventually has to get to us and eat us out. Just like when we throw a ball against the wall, it will come back at us. It's gonna happen.

This is what the *Work Manual* says about it: 'You can't fool God so don't make a fool of yourself. **You will harvest what you plant.** If you follow your selfish desires you will harvest destruction but if you follow the Spirit you will harvest eternal life' (Galatians 6:7-8).

Yes, I'm getting super-spiro again! But this one goes deep. If you plant bitterness, it will come back at you. You harvest what you plant.

Where is the Bloke Upstairs while our hearts are getting smashed?

People say to me, 'Watto, how could you possibly believe in and trust the Big Fella when you had three big hits in your early years?'

As well as the deaths of my mother and sister, at a young age I was subject to sexual interference by a supposedly trusted person in a church. I could have blamed 'God' for it all.

As strange as it might appear, I never once said, 'God, why did you let this happen to me?'

Even though I didn't really know the Big Fella back then, I was always looking for the 'more' part of me. The part you can't manufacture in your head. **My question was: who am I deep down and what's my purpose?**

> The answers kept coming that there was more to life
>   than just me.
>   I shouted out to the person I called 'God',
>   and I asked him to show me
>   in my life
>   if he was for real
>   or was he just a fairytale.

The more I asked him the more he showed me that he had a plan for me, and that he doesn't go around stuffing up my life or anyone else's in this world.

> That he brings me alive within
> and lights me up
> to do a turbocharged life
> with his power in my heart.

So from all this internal pain from my grief he has given me freedom to overcome and get on with it, and he allows me to encourage you if you're into a hard part of life.

Getting rid of the gunk

Sometimes you might think things are pretty tough and bad. You can stay there forever. Lots of blokes do.

I'm saying straight out: it's not an excuse. Face up to the facts.

The *Work Manual* has this to say: 'If you have sinned, you should **tell each other what you have done.** Then you can pray for one another and be healed. The prayer of an innocent person is powerful, and it can help a lot' (James 5:16).

Spit it out to a trusted bloke. Tell him all your gunk, whether you think it's your fault or someone else's. Spill your guts so you can be healed, freed, and more-become the real-deal bloke you were created to be.

I've seen this work many times. If a bloke can open up and talk it through with a trusted bloke, most of the time he'll sort it out. If he can speak it out loud and hear himself, he'll usually come up with the right decision.

There are plenty of good blokes around, not far away from you. Is there someone that you know in your gut that you can trust? He will give you the encouragement you need, the nudge to just kickstart you to get rid of the gunk. If you don't know anyone like that, think about joining a shed group or going to shednight.com.

Talking to a trusted bloke works. **It works for me and countless other blokes I've spoken to over the years.** It just works.

Getting free of the past

So, how do we right those wrongs from the past? Jesus died to set you free of all that crap to give you a clean and new heart, to be able to love and be loved. Does our society say that happens? No. Do I know it happens? Yes, because I've seen it.

If bitterness and hatred and unforgiveness are eating you out, ask yourself: 'Do I have a talk to the Big Fella about this?' You don't have to tell anyone else you're doing it. For a long time, I talked to God privately. Back then, I would have hated to think that anyone knew I was talking to God! (It's not like that now…!)

Why not try it for yourself? Have a red-hot talk to the Big Fella and say, 'Show me what's my hang up. What's screwing me up?'

Afterwards, you will see things you hadn't thought about before. Then you can ask him to take whatever it is and give you freedom. You can continue to become the real-deal champion. You won't spit the dummy. You'll see it through to the champion team.

You might have heard of the Lord's Prayer that's been said down through the ages. It's a Christian prayer the Big Fella gave everyone to pray to him. It says 'forgive us as we forgive others'. **The blueprint is for us to do the forgiving first, and then we can be free.**

If you don't believe God is for real, have a deep, deep think about your past and see what comes to the front of your mind. Have a really good look at it. Somehow or other you're going to have to let it go. Write it down and do your best to let it go forever out of your head and your heart and your spirit.

Dump all your garbage and get freedom!

As I was able to let go of my sadness, bitterness, resentment, unforgiveness and judgemental attitudes, the other person also was able to change. It wasn't a competition any more, or trying to get square. It was freedom!

How much easier for me to function in other areas of my life, when my head was happier and free of this hatred and bitterness!

I could have let my attitude kill my dreams and eat out my happiness if I had held onto this stuff. I chose to let my Creator do another inside job on my turbocharged heart and soul, so my head could let go of the resentment that was burning me up.

Have you got rocks around your heart?

I had no control over getting knocked down by grief from the deaths of my mother and my sister. It smashed my heart, robbing it of the nurture love from my mother that had made me flourish in my childhood.

I put rocks around my heart so no-one could get in and smash it again. I could give love easily but I didn't realise that **I couldn't take love into my smashed heart too well. I was too bitter, too unforgiving and holding on to too much resentment.**

But I'm a champion because I avoided this knockout and kept getting back up. I was able to ask the Creator of the universe: 'What is my struggle? Do I have hatred, bitterness, resentment or unforgiveness?' **He smashed the rocks around my heart** and dumped them at the cross where Jesus died. He gave me a new heart. Onward and upwards!

I took charge of the mess in my life. I refused to let it take me off the champion list. I opened up the gates of my heart to get a job done from the inside out.

You know, if we let go on the inside – our heart soul and spirit – a lot of those medical problems and mind ailments like anxiety and depression can be conquered. I reckon a lot of our cancers and diseases happen because our smashed emotions have weakened our immune system.

What's the key to letting go? If you're ready to find out whether the Big Fella is for real or not, ask him what's eating you out. Speak it out loud to a trusted bloke and take the 'getting fixed up' promise seriously. Get on with life.

If you sort this one out, you get rid of the painful stuff. **In its place comes joy, happiness, trust, encouragement and the ability not to be judgemental towards others.** You start to feel like a million dollars.

The take-home message

Do you want to become the real-deal champion you were created to be? The Creator of the Universe knew you before you were born, and he did not make you a junk bloke.

This is not rocket science. It's relational, connective stuff with the Creator who made us and who has a plan for you and me to set us on the road to victory. His plan isn't to stuff us up with roots of hatred, bitterness, resentment and unforgiveness. In lots of cases the battle may take time, so that layer by layer the bitterness can be shed, never to return.

And then eventually it happens – freedom. That's the take-home trophy. Keep asking for freedom. The Big Fella will hear you and help you from the inside out.

Inch by inch is a cinch; yard by yard can be too hard. Just go for a little bit at a time. Keep grinding away. You'll get there, step by step.

Hatred, bitterness, resentment and unforgiveness come back to bite big-time if you don't sort them out. But you can do it. Open up and let God, champion!

TO REMEMBER...

It's OK to have a little pity party or feel sorry for yourself from time to time.

Hatred, bitterness, resentment and unforgiveness are like a pimple that grows into a boil and busts.

Unforgiveness eventually will eat you out, like rust.

Spill your guts and be healed.

Some things will take a while to forgive, and some things can't ever be sorted out they way you might like. Just let it go to determine your destiny of champion freedom and victory!

BONUS:

Some red-hot tips from the *Work Manual*:

> Stop being bitter and angry and mad at others. Don't yell at one another or curse each other or ever be rude. Instead, **be kind and merciful, and forgive others**, just as God forgave you because of Christ. (Ephesians 4:31-32)

> **Try to live at peace with everyone!** Live a clean life. If you don't, you will never see the Lord. Make sure that no-one misses out on God's wonderful kindness. Don't let anyone become bitter and cause trouble for the rest of you. (Hebrews 12:14-15)

> Jesus said: Don't judge others, and God won't judge you. **Don't be hard on others, and God won't be hard on you**. Forgive others, and God will forgive you. (Luke 6:37)

> God loves you and has chosen you as his own special people. So be gentle, kind, humble, meek, and patient. **Put up with each other, and forgive anyone who does you wrong**, just as Christ has forgiven you. (Colossians 3:12-13)

4. Champions listen

> **TO GET YOU STARTED**
>
> Are you so darn busy that you haven't got time to listen properly? Does your woman say things like: You never listen to me, I told you that 2 days ago?
>
> 'Take the cotton wool out of your ears and shove it down your gob so you can listen.'
>
> Come on fellas! We can help each other get the gold out of listening the champion way.

Listen and cruise!

When I started my business, I loved the novelty of my truck. I could sit on 100kph with an 8 tonne load. Away I'd go, trying to get one extra load each day and going so hard I was pumping.

And then my old truckie mates told me to **get smart and drive to a plan.** You get most of the lights and you use less fuel when you're driving smart.

All I had to do was listen to those very experienced blokes and take it in. Know the lanes that don't pull you up all the time. No ripping, tearing and starting. Just cruise. Less fuel, less wear on the clutch and brakes, by just backing off at the right times.

I could do the same number of loads with less stress and get out at the end of the day as cool as a cucumber. They were offering me the benefit of their many years on the road. I just had to listen and take it in.

I had to keep the ears open.

I soon realised that the part of my truck driving job I loved most was getting out and dealing with people. I looked forward

to any opportunity to make a connection for more follow-on business. To do that, **I had to listen for the opportunities that people give you every day. If you keep your wits about you, you learn to hear what people are really saying.**

Talking when I should have been listening

Let me tell you about the day I got my nose splattered all over my face.

I used to think I was pretty tough, playing football. I'd play fullback, so I'd be on the gun full-forward. We'd be verbally abusing and niggling at each other all day – just part of the fun!

One day, the full-forward, much larger than me, **never said a word. And I didn't 'listen' to that!**

I was mouthing off, carrying on, telling him what I was going to do to him. When I went for the ball the next time he just went smash! straight in the nose, and I saw stars.

I went back on the field for the last quarter with blood everywhere and cotton wool stuffed up my nose. The opposition didn't have 18 any more, I could see 36 of them!

The moral of that story: Watto, you were talking when you should have been listening. **If I'd been listening instead of talking, I wouldn't have got that smack in the nose.**

Not listening kills relationships

Too often a bloke thinks he knows what's going on in his woman's head. He tries to read her mind.

If we just shut up and listen to her with all our heart, we hear the really true feelings of the problem. Then we can exchange our feelings. The woman will listen to you because you listened to her. Too often man thinks he has to solve the problem and he's in charge of things.

I've learned this in the university of hard knocks. I've tried to read my wife Margaret's mind. One day she said, 'I don't want you to fix it, all I want you to do is listen to me!' And you know what? When I did shut up and listen to her, I went, '**Wow, gee I've got a clever wife.**' Usually you can solve the problem if you listen to each other.

It's critical to listen to your children, too. If you don't listen to each one of them, some can miss out. The quiet children can miss out completely and shut down. The dominating personality can take the floor all the time and the others just tag along.

It's vital to get with your own son or daughter in a simple way and really listen to their hearts and feelings. If you're going to make a big decision as a family, make sure you talk to all your children, and find out what they think about it.

Fear blocks our ears

When blokes get in the truck at my truck driver training depot, the first, second and third lessons are the hardest with the Road Ranger gearbox. It's high stress.

Lots of times in these early lessons, blokes can have great difficulty in listening. Sometimes as an instructor you have to repeat the instruction many different times in many different ways until they finally hear it. It's like the penny drops.

There's nothing wrong with a bloke, but **he usually lets other things crowd his mind** such as: I feel like an idiot, I should be able to do this, I'm nervous, how am I going to go, what's the instructor going to think of me if I can't do it, I wonder if other blokes feel this dumb doing this.

All these things just rush in and blank out our listening. Sometimes we even swear abnormally and don't realise it.

The student needs calmness and an affirming word and no comparisons to anybody else.

Then the bloke can get on with it. He can accelerate his learning because he's overcome that inward pain. The listening becomes easier. As the lessons go on the student can think and work it out for himself and really feel like he's conquered the mountain.

Do you get nervous and worry about feeling like an idiot, and let it stop you listening?

Relax and listen. Be careful not to let these within-things blank out what matters in the situation. **You're a champion. The Creator didn't make you a junk person.**

Be an aggressive listener

When I talk about an 'aggressive listener', I don't mean someone who's angry! It's a bloke who's ready to work hard to make sure he really hears what the other person is saying. He keeps eye and heart contact, and has a single focus.

> Keep your antennas up.
>   There's usually more
>   and deeper.
>   To get to the story
>   you must   listen,
>   listen,
>   listen
>   and you will get it eventually.

Take care at the start of all connections that you hear and listen. Show genuine interest and don't rush when you meet a person, so you can remember their name. Everyone likes to hear their own name, so try to lock it in your memory straight off. Listen hard!

4. CHAMPIONS LISTEN

> There's always more to the story
> and you'll get it
> if you listen with your head
>   and your heart.
> Don't rush.
>   You can learn to listen.
>   It doesn't always come naturally.

See, I talk a lot but I'm also listening at the same time, because I reckon I can do three things at once, ha ha!

Listen for opportunities

I had left the comfort of 22 years of security as a clerk and was rolling along nicely in my one-man business of tipper truck owner/driver, delivering soil, sand and gravel.

I had my name and phone number on my truck door, but the honeymoon was over. I was too much alone in my truck cabin all day. **I love being with people and when I realised that it was just going to be me in the cabin all day every day, I wanted some new challenges.**

At this time I was just starting to get to know the Bloke Upstairs. Once he got me on my own in the truck with no-one else to distract me, he and I could chat. I needed time to get to know him so I could trust him, and the days in the truck gave me that time.

I was confined again, this time not to a desk but to a truck cabin. I thanked the Big Fella for giving me freedom from sitting behind a desk, but now I was ready for more action. I told him I'd get very bored doing this for the rest of my working life.

I asked him whether or not he had some more excitement or another opportunity for me – whether he had a plan for me. See if you can guess what happened next.

Listen to strangers

Back then, you could get a truck licence without needing a car licence first. Our eldest son, Haydn, turned 17 – driving age – and he learned to drive the truck. He asked me to take him in the tipper truck for his practical test at the Petrie police station in Brisbane's northern suburbs. Haydn's success gave his school mates ideas. It started a run of his mates each doing up to 10 hours training with me in the truck, and then testing at Petrie on a Friday afternoon, the last truck licence assessment of the week.

I seemed to be always going to the Petrie police station. The test time is one hour, so this enabled me to have a sleep under the big leopard tree at the front of the courthouse!

During one of those many naps, a total stranger came up to me and said, 'How much is your hourly rate in your truck? You're always over here. **Why don't you become a truck driving trainer?'**

He said he was a long time car instructor. He said the area didn't have a truck driving school and could do with one. He'd kept his eye on me teaching Haydn and his mates, while doing his car instructing.

As you could expect from an Aussie male, I didn't give too much information away. I was totally ignorant of what a truck driving school meant, but reluctantly took the business card he offered. I was only half listening, thinking, *What's he on about?*

He also offered to help me out with training and said to just give him a call. Can you believe it?

I really didn't listen carefully because my inherited response was not to give anything away. Most of the time we think, *What does this sticky-beak want?* The problem: talking and thinking when I should have been listening!

I'd been asking for challenge and adventure but I didn't see it when it came to me. Where did I want or expect the answer to come from? A business coach? A motivational book? My focus was like a dot on a page. You can spend all your time looking at the dot, and you don't realise it's on a big page. I was limiting my thinking.

It was a test. My first response was to give a guarded, pride-generated answer and act like I didn't really need anything. The real test was still to come: what I was going to do with this opportunity?

Do I just bash ahead and hope for the best and hope I drop into the champion's club? Or is there a better way? Sure is! Ask the Creator of the universe for the opportunity or dream and be prepared to listen and hear.

Don't restrict where the answer may come from.

The tried and proven *Work Manual for the Champion Life* says: 'Be sure to welcome strangers into your home. By doing this, some people have welcomed angels as guests, without even knowing it' (Hebrews 13:2).

Get it? I could have missed this opportunity because I didn't know this bloke. Listen, listen, listen. To strangers!

Shut up and listen!

So yes! I did phone the stranger and yes, I did take up his generous offer. His name was Don. I did the time in the back seat of Don's car learning how to train from him. 22 years later **I am telling you a little story that contains a big tip in helping you make the champion's team.**

Don is now 81 years old and he still encourages me, so you can see what happens when you listen and hear the right idea or encouragement from someone who you can respect. And it just may be a total stranger!

Don's idea and the Big Fella's promise has developed into the premier truck driver training centre on the northside of Brisbane, training and encouraging thousands of blokes and women in obtaining a truck licence. Today we operate 6 trucks in all classes.

Yes! I did the hard yards 60 hours per week, 6 days a week for 16-odd years. But now I tell you of the immense gain. Where would I be if I hadn't listened to Don?

And it was more than driver training. **I always wanted to teach blokes, but the Bloke Upstairs said, 'I want you to do it one-on-one in a truck cabin.'** I've spoken to many thousands of blokes that way.

Now I get to talk to lots more men at shed groups around Australia, and on the radio. That's talking to a lot of people! I can see that during those years I was being trained for what I do today, encouraging blokes.

And all I had to do was shut up and listen to Don. And take it in and think about where it fitted into my world. When I commenced this part of my journey with the phone call to the stranger, I couldn't see the prize at the end of the race. The results are history, all because I listened to this bloke and let it develop.

Shut up and listen to the Big Fella

I first started to chat with the Big Fella back when I was trucking gravel. I didn't hear his voice at first – probably because of the truck engine noise, ha ha. At that stage of my being the real-deal I didn't have a clue who he was.

I was pretty sure God was for real by then, but I wouldn't dare tell anyone else. It was quite comfy having my little 'please help me God' prayers – mainly when I was up the creek without a paddle because something had gone wrong with my business or my life.

Little did I realise that before I could move on in my business and my real-deal life, **I needed to be all alone with him in my truck cabin for 10-12 hours each day so I could learn to shut up and listen to him.**

But things settled in my head and started to stick. **I could think and listen without interruption and started to trust him.** I learned he had a plan for me, not to stuff things up but to kick me along.

I couldn't talk publicly about it. I was too full of my own importance and ego. I was all-over-the-shop, trying so hard to be accepted. **I still thought it was all about me instead of all about him – the Creator.**

Good friends gave me a wall hanging with a picture of an old country shed, and written down the bottom from the *Work Manual* was this: 'My God shall supply all my needs according to his riches in glory (Philippians 4:19)'. **I read it and it stuck in my head. I 'listened' to my Creator. That gem is still in my head today, and it still works.**

I 'charged off into the black night', even though there were many things I couldn't guarantee. I just set out to **do my best and let God do the rest.** It's still working 30 years later. But I had to listen to him and hear what he said to me.

> **Do you need a safe and non-judgemental and secure place like I did to learn to listen?**

He will show you how you can hear from him in so many ways, but it will be between you and him.

So mate, it gets down to you and me, and where we're at with the big picture of life. Gently, gently start to look squarely at who you are, and see that you're OK. The champion in you is the one when no-one is looking – when we're real with warts and all. **That's the one that's really you. As we listen more to other champions, we really come alive.**

Gee it's nice to know that God knows all the crap the world has dumped on us throughout our lives. He knows that we haven't a clue about being the real-deal. **He just stays with us – no dramas. He's always there for us.**

Stop listening to the wrong people

Being a typical Aussie bloke, at the beginning I would keep my talks with the Bloke Upstairs very private – just between him and me. I felt like I would be seen as 'wussy' to actually be talking publicly about God, especially as a truckie.

About this time a special lady who was inspirational for my life skills gave me a sticker that said: 'Truckin' for Jesus'. Because of pride or call it what you like, I didn't have the guts to put this sticker on show. So I put it high on the inside sunshade in the cabin, just for me and the Big Fella to know about, a people-pleasing decision. I could tell my friend, 'Yes, I have the sticker on my truck,' but keep it as a personal thing for my Creator and me. It was always embarrassing when some stranger got in the cab or stood outside in a position where they could read 'Truckin' for Jesus'.

I can look back now and say that I wasn't being the real-deal about this. **I thought I needed people's approval – but what I needed was knowing for real my Creator's plan for me.** I spent too much time listening to the wrong people and worrying about their opinions. **I needed to go straight to the top. No middleman.**

I was listening to people who didn't understand the heart of a real-deal bloke. They didn't really care about me, so why was I seeking their approval?

It was like when I was first talking about buying the truck, and everyone in the office had opinions. I worried about things they said to me. Once I got out and actually started doing the job, any of the negative things they'd said to me were nothing. They didn't have a clue!

It's the same with talking to the Big Fella. Some people will say negative things about it, but it's only because they don't understand it. Once you start finding out for yourself, you'll wonder why you ever worried about their opinions.

Come on! It's all about being real. When you get to be more who you are, you can listen to people's big ideas about what you believe, and then you can go away and put the billy on, have a cup of tea and think: *Is what they said for real? No, it's a bit stupid.*

The take-home message

God really has a great sense of humour. He gives us these little moments throughout our lives to get us to listen to his ways.

Take care not to restrict where it comes from. Don the driving instructor started out a stranger, and 22 years later is a close and loyal friend, and one of my inspirations to becoming the real-deal champion.

Become an aggressive listener. Don't miss a word. Let it sit in your head, take it into your heart, and then let it come out. Don't rush. Just keep the antennas up and open.

Do you want a new challenge and adventure? Maybe it's already there, if you listen to the right people.

Are you listening? Are you really hearing?

Listen and take it in.

TO REMEMBER...

Take the cotton wool out of your ears and shove it in your mouth and listen.

Be an aggressive listener.

Keep your antennas up. There's always more to the story.

Listen to the total stranger, total stranger, total stranger. Listen, listen, listen!

BONUS:

A couple more gems from the *Work Manual* – how true are these!

> Fools think they know what is best, but **a sensible person listens to advice.** (Proverbs 12:15)

> My dear friends, you should be **quick to listen and slow to speak** or to get angry. (James 1:19)

> It's **stupid and embarrassing to give an answer before you listen.** (Proverbs 18:13)

5. Champions emerge from knowing about the Bloke Upstairs to knowing him

TO GET YOU STARTED

Does your head feel so tight it's like it's in a vice that's getting tighter and tighter?
Does the world tell you you're good and capable, but you don't feel that way?
Are you asking: 'Who am I, and why?'
Are you asking: 'Is there more than this?'

Are you asking yourself: 'Is there such a thing as God?'

Life can roll along OK, but if you really want to know whether there's more, looking for the 'wow' part of who you are, then that comes from knowing where you come from.

Champion, let's look at our true identity.

Knowing about vs really knowing

I know Simon Black, the champion Brisbane Lions AFL footballer. (A bit of name-dropping!) I've got to know how many games he's played, all his statistics. I've only actually spoken with him personally a dozen-odd times. So yes, I know him, but no, I don't really know him well. **We can know about a person without really knowing the person.**

It's the same with the Big Fella. **We can know all about him, study and know the Bible, but not know him on a one-on-one, first-name basis.** Now that I really know him, I can trust him. I can let him have my spirit so he can do a 'job' on the inside of me, and keep me the real-deal.

If you have doubts about the Bloke Upstairs as to whether he's for real, that's OK. **At different times in my life I sure had doubts. But I was lost in religious 'stuff' and didn't know the person it was all about.** No-one ever introduced me to him. They just told me about him – and mostly about how to do 'church' and why.

Knowing for yourself

There was a day in my 30s when I asked my Creator to show me in my life whether he was for real or whether he was just a fairytale. At that time we lived on a property, and I went out into the backyard, looked up into the sky and yelled out to him.

5. CHAMPIONS EMERGE FROM KNOWING ABOUT THE BLOKE UPSTAIRS TO KNOWING HIM

I needed to know in my life – nobody else's! Not my wife's or my Grandma's life. I had to know inside me, not just in my head.

I wasn't in some deep hole of despair, like a marriage bust-up or just lost a job or had some medical hit. **I had simply reached the moment in manhood where I needed to know: was it all about me, or was there more?** It was a time when I felt a deep call within me.

I believe no-one proves to anyone else that God is for real. There's a saying that goes like this: 'A man convinced against his will remains the same man still'.

You see some things, and hear plenty of others. You can know all the words in the Bible back to front, but the real crunch comes when you hit the wall in your own life, and realise you need to make a choice. **Will you open or shut the door to the Big Fella?**

Words don't necessarily convince anyone. But once **you get to know him yourself, you'll soon recognise him in the lives of others who follow him.**

You'll get to know that they have made that same choice to believe in him and accept his ways. That's the key to life.

Dead or alive?

There was another time when **I got a wake-up call about my spirit.** It came from an unexpected person at a surprising time and place.

This bloke came to list our house for sale. He saw a Bible on the shelf, and the particular version was called the *Living Bible*. He said, 'Whose Bible is that?' I said, 'Oh that's Margaret's.' **He said, 'Well is it living? Do you open it?'** I was getting a bit steamed-up by now, thinking, *Who do you think you are to ask me these questions?*

He said, 'If you don't open it, you're spiritually dead.'

That hit me like a tonne of bricks. 'Who do you think you are?' I said. 'I know about God. I went to Sunday School.' I felt like punching his head in.

But he just said, 'Your spirit's dead.'

After he left, I told Margaret, 'I don't want him back in this house. What right did he have to come and say that?'

He hit a note and stirred up anger in me. I wanted to tell him to ping off. **But from that day that little jolt didn't leave my mind, until I came to know that I am more than body and mind – I have a spirit as well, and it needs to be connected to the Big Fella to come alive.**

Now I'm glad he said it. Otherwise how would I know? You don't often hear that at Sunday morning church. **You hear it in reality where the rubber hits the road.**

Twenty years later, I've said a similar thing to lots of blokes around Australia: you're either spiritually alive or you're dead, it's one or the other.

No-one misses out on the battle

I heard a panel on the radio debating atheism and God and the church. It was all head stuff, nothing from the heart. I thought: *What a waste of time. They've proven nothing.*

I felt like getting on the phone and asking them, 'What about where I go in my life? Come and meet people whose lives are totally transformed because they have met him for real.' **You can argue with a bloke's theology, but you can't argue with his story. That's what Shed Happens is all about.**

Fellas, we'll do life and it's all rosy and cosy for a while, but no-one misses out on the battle. It's just a different time and a different nametag. **So when we get to the battle, and we ask: who am I and why?, then we've got to go outside of ourselves.** That's when we're more likely to ask if there is such a thing as God.

I defy the smartest bloke in town to say, 'I've got life worked out.' We never really get it all together. We're pretty good after the event at coming up with the theories, but we're not so good before the event. We're so smart that when the tsunami hits we can work out why it hits. But why can't we get our computers out, and make it go back the other way? **There's so many other things we can't control, in depression and health for example. We can't even get the weather forecast right. But we never stop and ask the Bloke who's in charge of the weather for advice!**

When things are going well it seems like we can work out every great plan and deal for ourselves. But even when life is good, there is more to life than that.

Once you get to know the Big Fella you think about life in a different way. He knew me before I was born, he knows every hair on my head, he blew the first breath into me.

Why was it so hard for me to get to know him?

I'm not talking about 'church' and 'religion' here, fellas – this mob or that mob. I'm only talking about the Creator of the universe. Is he for real? **Have you got to the point where you're calling out to find out whether he's for real in your life?** When you get to this point, there's something more in your life that will come out of the 'within' part of you.

The new *Work Manual*?

In the past, whether or not you believed in God, the greater majority of people in Australia grew up with and chose to live by the Ten Commandments. Our society was founded on such principles as 'Do not kill', 'Do not steal', 'Do not commit adultery'. The saying 'Do unto others as you would have them do to you' – which originally came from Jesus – was well-known and respected.

But in recent times it seems that those who influence the world are hell-bent on another set of standards for living.

It's not my first choice to change everything, but I'm not anti-change. I like to consider the facts first and see how it fits, and then take what seems the best option.

So OK, if we're going to get rid of the old, then surely there's got to be a new 'set of rules' or a new set of standards coming out of the new 'bible'.

Where is it?

I'd like to take a look for myself and see it it's worth throwing out the old for the new. **I can't find the new *Work Manual*! I can't find anyone who has a copy.** In life as in work, sooner or later we have to refer to the manual. So what do we refer to now?

The good guts of the Bible has been pushed aside by the unidentified influences of our society, the mysterious 'they', but no-one has produced the new guidelines where we can hold it in our hands.

So what's going on? Where do we really sit with all the new ideas on how to do life? Do you like the way our society is changing? Do you like the way people treat each other and the things you hear on the news? Some things are just too good ever to be replaced! The old *Work Manual* has so many gems to help us in everyday life.

Choices a bloke makes without realising

For me, **knowing the Big Fella was the main thing I had to work through with lots of blood, sweat and tears to** eventually discover that it was the clincher. It made all the difference for me. But read on and have a sort out for yourselves.

Now remember I'm not talking about religion or some denominational thing. I'm not knocking churches either. It's just not about that. I don't want you to be put off or confused. **It's not a building or a way of doing it. This is all about a relationship with our Creator.**

I used to think I had to look after my brain and my body, but I didn't know what to do about my spirit, the part that's not just physical or mental.

The body: I do exercise and try to eat well and go to the naturopath and take all these pills (but I get bored doing it like most blokes) and Margaret tells me I look OK.

The mind: I try to take in the news of the day, and read and learn and continue to develop my brain, and keep up with what's going on around me.

The spirit: Previously, **I didn't have a clue how to get my spirit to come alive!** I had done nothing to develop my spirit because I had shut that door.

Eventually I had that talk to the Bloke Upstairs, God. He gave me my spirit and **so I asked him to do a job on me – not too harshly as I didn't want to turn into some holy roller or a super-spiro.** So bit-by-bit he began tuning up my spirit, so that my head could think better and differently and I could become more real. He still does this and I am a continuing work-in-progress.

I let go of control and courageously asked my Creator to do whatever he had to do to give me an alive spirit. He made my spirit come alive. Hope you are getting an inside track to this absolute stunner!

Yes, for most men **we've been raised and conditioned to use our heads and work it out.** Use your head and **keep that turbocharged spirit in its shy place.** Don't dare talk about God, let alone his son Jesus, and, ah, well, no-one talked about God's Spirit, so we grew up ignorant. Spirits were scotch, rum and vodka, and Jesus had been wussy-ised by society as some limp-wristed loser.

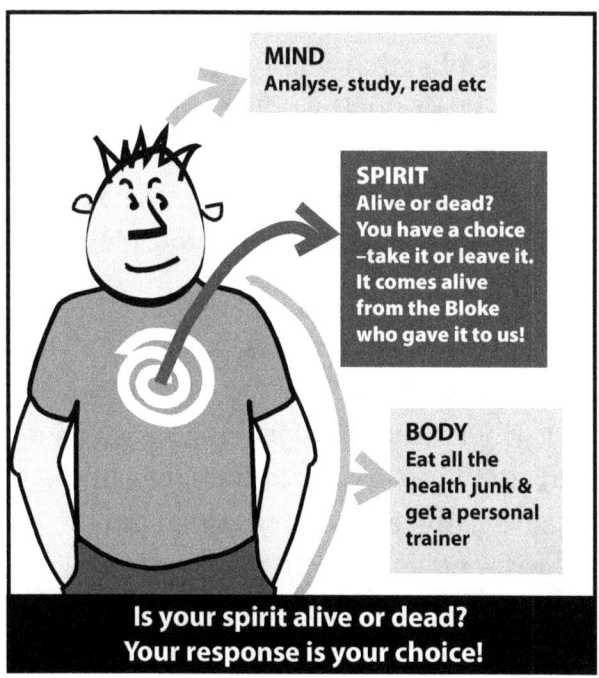

That's not what I found when I asked the Big Fella to show me how real he was in my life. That's why I want to make sure you **don't get conned** and this real stuff is handed on.

You need to get the full message, both sides of the story, so you can make a choice.

Half the story

I don't think men have got the full story about God, and the relationship of God and Jesus, so we're making a decision on only half the facts. You don't have to do it my way, but I want to give you the opportunity to have a look at this before you make your own choice.

Fellas, remember that when we hear something new and unfamiliar often there will be ridicule and rejection within us before acceptance. We've been conditioned and taught not to trust. We think someone's trying to take advantage of us. **But don't let other people decide for you. Make up your own mind.**

I grew up thinking God was the Big Boss with all the rules, taking the fun out of life. God was for Sunday, for a couple of hours where you didn't get too excited. Sunday School was boring, and I was always in trouble with the teacher! It was very sad at Easter about them killing Jesus on a cross, and Christmas was Santa mixed with carols and this little baby in a dirty manger, presents and holidays.

5. CHAMPIONS EMERGE FROM KNOWING ABOUT THE BLOKE UPSTAIRS TO KNOWING HIM

The image I had of **Jesus was this young bloke with long hair wearing a white dress and maybe a sheep over his shoulder, with a face that was nonplussed bordering on sad.** His name didn't sound like a bloke's name to me. (I didn't know back then that lots of blokes in South America are called Jesus.)

I didn't relate him to the reality of manhood and life that we encounter every day. I'm sad to think that I took so long to get to know that this bloke is the best example of the champion's way of life. He's also the reason we can have a champion life in the first place.

What has been served up to blokes over my lifetime is only a fraction of the message about the reality of God and Jesus. **We haven't been given the relationship message about the best mate you can have.** On one side, we were given rules and don'ts and negatives. On the other side, we were told to love a man, which generally doesn't sit well with blokes.

We've been sold a dummy.

There's more to God than rules, and more to Jesus than the fluffy-duck soft part where a lot of people want to keep him.

Jesus the Bloke was a carpenter, a chippie. He told these boofheads to follow him, and none of them could seem to get it right, but he didn't give up on them. He gave turbocharged words that blasted people into the champion's team. He wasn't afraid of anyone. He took on injustice and greed. He did real life and set up the perfect way of doing life, kind and gentle sometimes, and other times playing the hard ball and stepping up to the plate. Most blokes have an instinct to want to save the world, but he actually did it. **We've been robbed of all this because he's been wussy-ised into nothingness.**

This bloke was The Bloke. He was the All. He was the Real-Deal. Fellas we haven't been given the real guts of this, because when you get to know this bloke called Jesus, there's nothing wussy about him.

Cut out the middleman

Over the past 23 years of training people to drive a heavy rigid truck, that usually meant 8–12 one-on-one hours of blood, sweat and tears before the victory was gained and the licence obtained. I would have easily tallied up 60,000 one-on-one hours with blokes in the truck.

You can get to know someone and to be trusted in 8-12 hours. **The Aussie bloke is a real one-on-one bloke** and if he knows he's not going to be judged, and he feels he's in a safe place with you, he's usually comfortable to open up his heart on some issue. Let's face it, **where do you find that sort of a place, fellas – somewhere you can call it as it is and know you're not going to be bashed for it? That's rare and special in this day and age.**

Well, the truck cabin with a 15-speed gear lever between us has been a special place for many blokes to off-load some stuff. A question that's always been comfortable for me to ask of all blokes in the truck is, 'Do you have any faith and belief in the Big Fella?'

Way, way up in the high 90% they say, 'Yes.'

'But' – here it comes – 'I don't go to church.'

I say, 'I didn't ask you about church. I asked you about God,' and they again say, 'Yes, I do believe in God.'

When they ask me what church I go to, I say, 'I'm not telling you, because that leads to fault-finding about church and people and things that have turned people off from knowing God. So we get shoved off the most important person you could ever meet and get sidetracked into stuff that is just stuff and doesn't do anyone any good.'

Again, I'm not against 'church', I just don't want you to get distracted by things that might have happened in the past. Church really is a gathering of people – all in the process of getting to know that they are champions – and it can be great.

Fellas, champions, **don't get sidetracked! Go to the top – no middleman!**

Don't let other people decide for you

One of my great mates grew up being told by his stepdad, 'Don't worry about God. There's no such person and it's all rubbish. You'll end up in a box in the ground like everyone else, full of maggots. There's no such thing as heaven. And women are just there to be used.'

Well his life based on that entry into manhood has produced disaster in all areas. After 40 years of despair, he got to the point of life and death and he cried out, '**If there's a God up there I sure need to know, otherwise I die!**'

Four years on, after meeting his Creator, **he now has a new life and he's been able to repair lots of previous pain and heartache with his family.** There's still more work to do, but he now lives a new life in victory, with his Creator as his guide. He helps others in similar holes to where he came from.

> **It wasn't about how much Bible he knew
> or what tradition he followed.
> It was just plain old-fashioned
> going straight to the top,
> no middleman,
> no diversions,
> and no   frills,
> bells or whistles
> or fairy floss.**

Just meet the Big Fella and let him teach you how to trust him and seek his ways of doing life for your future. **He's got on-the-job training with a turbocharged boost.**

My mate can now say, '**Watto, once I lived a 1-cent life and didn't know that there was a $100-note life.** Wow, since I've got to know the Big Fella I feel like I'm in heaven every day and have a $100 life.'

Why did my mate have to go through life conditioned by the wrong father/son teaching? He was schooled in a self-centred way of life with no respect for God or for women. **What he sowed he reaped in constant disaster, until in desperation he met his Creator. He cried out 'God, help!' and opened his rocky, smashed heart. He now knows hope and has a future.**

No-one will force you to do this. You've gotta wanna! This man did, because it was life or death to him.

My family

My mother and grandmother really went for God, Jesus and church. My father, no!

He was anti, because when he was a boy he was a nobody who wasn't allowed to sit up the front of the church. The front pews were partitioned off and saved for the so-called 'important people'. He had to sit behind the chains.

He also kept telling me not to marry a Catholic. Funny that he didn't ever tell me why, and I don't think he could have told me why, but I grew up thinking that Catholics were playing for the opposition.

I was taught to judge people without any evidence. Once again, stuff gets in the road. Later I got to learn that God loves people who call themselves Catholic just like he loves me. Some of my best friends are Catholic!

I reckon my Dad's in heaven because in his last moments in the hospital just before his spirit departed, he was sitting up with his hands in the praying position. The Creator calls us to himself all the way through our journey in life on earth, and as I said before we men have been taught, conditioned and expected to have shy spirits. Dad certainly was one of them. He would never publicly say he believed in God or anything like that, but in the latter part of his life something changed.

God knows what we're really thinking. I believe there's going to be a lot of men in heaven who didn't have the guts to speak up about knowing God.

The society we live in keeps us quiet on our spiritual thoughts. I can't see the advantage of it. If we heard more of each other's thoughts it would help us determine the big picture of life on the road to becoming real. We could encourage each other more.

Remember, no-one forces you to believe. Don't let them force you not to believe, either.

We men ain't made stupid, even though our television shows can make us feel that way. Lots of blokes think they're never going to make it. But that can change right now. **Drop off the world's way, turn off the TV, and have a talk to the Big Fella and come to your own conclusion.**

Stuff that gets in the way

I was deceived by 'stuff' – church traditions and styles of worship and things that some church people had done to me – and it kept me away from the personal thing with Jesus the carpenter. I couldn't accept that it was the manly thing to be in love with another man. Life screwed me up inside and I kept on trying to keep this idea down.

I never felt as though I could get into the 'club' at Margaret's church. Everyone seemed so serious – and no-one ever talked about footy. The church service seemed to me like a funeral. I sat up the back for a long time and no-one really made an effort to talk to me.

Baptism became a big issue for me. That's when you get washed with water as a symbol of belonging to the Big Fella – like a citizenship ceremony.

I had a problem with the church I went to in my early years. They believed in being totally dunked under the water, usually around the teenage years. Well, it didn't matter what the pastor said, I didn't want a bar of it. I couldn't hear what he was saying. All I could see was another man – a man who was respected in that church – who interfered with me sexually in my early years. I wasn't able to speak it out at that time in my life, so they didn't know about it and they couldn't do anything to fix it.

The Big Fella's messengers weren't getting through to my brain because I had developed distrust of Christians over the actions of this man. In no way did I want to be like him. I thought: *If that's how I would turn out giving my life to the Lord, then it isn't going to happen.* So I didn't get baptised.

Then when I got married I followed Margaret to the next 'mob' whose tradition was to christen (pour water on) babies, and so I'd missed it again, because I wasn't a baby any more!

I finally got baptised in my 30s with water from the kitchen tap and Margaret by my side. I call it the Squib's Baptism, because I didn't have the guts to stand up at the front of the church! I didn't feel like I fitted in.

My life was pretty cruddy at the time. There was something inside of me saying, 'Just get it done.' I had gotten so stitched up in the tradition and the style and trying to meet conditions of the thing called church, I wasn't sure which one was right and which one was wrong. But I finally just did it. Thankfully, the pastor wasn't locked in that it had to be done a certain way, so he was happy to do it at our house, and I was thankful for that.

So at the end of the day, did the baptism work, with water from the kitchen tap? Yes, because it was all about God, not about Watto or the water or the place. It was what he did on the inside of me.

I look back now and know my Creator let me experience all this confusion that prevented me from getting to know him, so I could tell men to just do it, just get baptised – in the ocean, the river, the bath. Use water and say those words and leave the consequences up to the Big Fella. It's all about him anyway, not about us!

Don't make hard work of God's business. He never meant it to be confusing or difficult.

See what I mean? For too long, 'stuff' got in the road of my relationship with the King of all champions. See how clouded and confused my head was with traditions, styles of how to sing, act and speak? It was all too confusing to me. I wanted action and reality. But I could use things and events and people as excuses to keep me away from Jesus. I was conned.

Why is it that we can't just get to meet God, our Creator, Jesus his Son and enjoy his Spirit? **Why have we let 'stuff' and disappointment and disgust with others and the world get in the road of the best and free-est way to do life?**

> If there's light, there's dark.
> If there's heaven, there's hell.
> If there's God, there's devil.
> If God is good, devil is bad.
> If God wants to give you life and eternity,
> the devil wants death and deceit.
> Deceit and the deceiver holds us back and clouds our thinking.
> God loves us. The devil hates us.

What about you?

Hopefully, in reading this chapter on the Champion of champions, you will identify some things that can cause you to keep your eyes off knowing the Big Fella on a first-name basis. **But it's never too late to change or learn. You've just gotta wanna!**

> As we become more the real-deal bloke
> > we can be open to see and hear more
> > > but not get rattled by differences.
> You can get to know that you are who you are,
> > and that's champion,
> > that's identity,
> and you can get to know Whose you are,
> > you belong to the Big Fella
> > and that's security,
> and your future is assured,
> > that's destiny
> > > because he has a plan to prosper you.

Now again, if you're not sure where you stand regarding God, champion, just have a red-hot talk with him and ask him to show you that he is for real.

Keep cool. Don't try to make anything happen. Don't try to get super-spiro. Don't play God.

He will show you in your life. Don't limit him. Don't try to tell God how to do his job. Hang in there and keep asking him to show you – and it will happen. It can come through many different ways and many different people.

No such thing as luck

So why have we made finding this most vital part of the champion within us so difficult? Why have we allowed the crap and deceit of the world to keep us shy and shielded from truth?

Don't make hard work of it. It's between you and your Creator and he knows your head, heart and motives anyway. He made you!

When you are asking the Bloke Upstairs to show you in your life if he's for real, you may think that what happens afterwards is just good luck or a fluke or circumstances. But hold fast, keep asking him.

God has a sense of humour and he likes to laugh with us. **He doesn't judge us in our questioning and he gives us another shot at it.** You'll eventually run out of flukes and circumstances and you'll get to know that there's no such thing as good luck. **It's all about your destiny.**

This is what the *Work Manual* says: '**For I know the plans I have for you,' declares the Lord, 'plans to prosper you and not to harm you, plans to give you hope and a future'** (Jeremiah 29:11 NIV). How good is this promise for champion assurance?

Don't get the guilts if you can't publicly recite Bible verses, don't know the history stories, haven't a clue about the strange dreams of Revelation and haven't read the book from cover to cover.

What I do is read the *Work Manual*, and if the Big Fella wants to stick a little gem in my brain and plant it in my heart, I go for it. He speaks into my spirit whenever I listen. The Bible is chock full of fantastic promises for you and me. He will give them to you as you ask – and they work!

I've grown to know that my Creator loves me and I have a dinky-di relationship with him. I can say I love God and put him first in my life.

The take-home message

> **Talk to the Big Fella about everything one-on-one, and that even includes your...**
> **footy   ute   woman**
> **music   study   farm   job**
> **whatever.**
> **Trust him with your future**
> **and know he gives you another go,**
> **irrespective of your past.**
> **And he loves**
> **even you –**
> **no strings attached.**

What I needed to do all along was just let go of the steering wheel of my life and let the Big Fella steer. He has given me spiritual 'spine'. He sets me on the champion course of destiny. I hope that it works out for you, too.

So, seek him first and watch out for a life of champion challenges and adventures.

This is the big one in the making of the real-deal champion. Hope you can get aboard. No one forces you to believe. You've gotta wanna!

> **TO REMEMBER...**
>
> If you do what you've always done, you'll
> get what you've always got.
>
> Get to know the Bloke Upstairs on a first-name basis.
> Cut out all the middlemen and all that distracts you.
>
> Aussies blokes are shy in spirit but God
> knows our hearts and motives anyway.
>
> Tell others your God-moments. They encourage.
>
> You'll run out of good luck, chances and flukes – there's
> no such thing! – and know it's all God's destiny.

BONUS:

Some gems from the *Work Manual*, when you're ready to find out some more...

Jesus said, 'A thief comes only to rob, kill, and destroy. **I came so that everyone would have life, and have it in its fullest.**' (John 10:10)

All who call out to the Lord will be saved. (Romans 10:13)

'I am the way, the truth, and the life!' Jesus [said]. 'Without me, no-one can go to the Father.' (John 14:6)

God loved the people of this world so much that he gave his only Son, **so that everyone who has faith in him will have eternal life and never really die.** (John 3:16)

6. Champions honour their father and mother, so that 'all goes well'

> **TO GET YOU STARTED**
>
> Are you holding things against your father or mother? Do you say, 'I'm never going to be like my father'? Have you cut your father or mother out of your life? If you have children are you wondering why they don't respect you?
>
> If you don't honour your parents, the one who loses is you. And then your own family loses too.
>
> But champion, we can turn this around! It's winnable! And there's a prize at the finish.

Are you a messed-up boy?

When we are growing for those first dozen years, fellas, **we are looking for something big in and from our parents, especially our father**, and we develop mindsets. We often build up resentments and disappointments, forgetting that there can be lots of positives along the way. We can make judgements that we justify by how the cards fell in our life.

We don't do anything to deserve some of the heartache and abuse that we are exposed to, but facts are facts. S*** happens. It's how we deal with it that counts.

The problem is not the test. How we deal with the problem is the real test.

There's so many screwed-up blokes who say about their father, 'I'm not going to talk to that bastard ever again in my life. I don't even want to know him.' Even though we may have been mistreated, that attitude just eats us out.

For all sorts of reasons, we blokes can become driven by the mindset that we're not going to be like our father. That was my problem. **I didn't want to be anything like my Dad.**

Resenting and hating our parents isn't the way to avoid making their mistakes. We seem to follow in their footsteps whether we like it or not. If you're going to buy a racehorse, you go and study the pedigrees, and look at the mother and the father, the grandmothers and the grandfathers. You look at the lines to see what a horse will be like – a sprinter or a stayer.

It's the same with people – we often see similar traits, habits and attitudes through the generations. A lot of blokes end up alcoholics like their father. If a boy sees his old man has got a porn stash, that makes it more difficult for the boy. How can he have a good normal sexual relationship if he has no respect for women?

You don't have to stay messed-up

We may have had a bad start, but the champion within us can emerge if we have a red-hot crack at the promises of the Creator of the universe.

This is what the *Work Manual* has to say about our parents: 'Honour (esteem and value as precious) your father and your mother—this is the first commandment with a promise—that all may be well with you and that you may live long on the earth.' (Ephesians 6:2-3, AMP). God said how we treated our parents was so important that he listed it among the top ten principles for real-deal life on earth – the Ten Commandments!

If 'all' is not going well with you, it's worth a look at how you are going with 'honour your father and mother'. Could the two be linked?

So you had a raw deal with your father. So you hate him, or you never want to be like him, or you don't want to cast eyes on him for the rest of your life, or he'll never get to meet his grandchildren.

Keep that sort of thinking and the only one who loses is you, not the old man who may have let you down. He may even be dead and buried, but **your deep pain lingers on if you are not able to honour his position as your father.**

Well, get over it! Honour means 'honour the fact that he was your old man' irrespective of every disappointing act he pulled on you or your mother or your family. **Honour the posi-**

tion. He was your father. **It doesn't say you have to accept any of his wrongdoing.**

We can wallow in the poop or we can pick ourselves up, dust ourselves off and get on with it. If it doesn't kill us, it can make us stronger and wiser. No pain, no gain! Come on, pull on your boots. It's game on! Get moving – it's worth it.

Watto as a messed-up boy

I was the only son in my family and I never felt like a champion when I was growing up. I've already told you how I went towards my mother's smother love, and **built up fear and resentment towards my father because he was always talking me down.** That's how I chose to take it aboard. He didn't want me to be a lair or a show-off, but he never talked it through with me.

OK, it didn't kill me and it was good for me in the end. He just thought it was his role to toughen me up. He did what he knew best. **I did not honour my dad in all ways, even though he was doing his best.** He was giving me his all and he was a good man, a good provider. **I made sure I developed a problem with him.**

My father's brother didn't have a son, so I became his little champion. He spoiled me rotten, so I liked him more than my father – not even realising that I had two men who loved me: my Dad and my uncle.

Later on, I got to see how that would have riled my Dad and made him jealous. **No-one spoke to me about what my Dad may be feeling.** No-one got into my heart to help me realise there was more to the story. No-one told me about honour. I only used the word at school when we 'honoured' the Queen.

My two wonderfully-loving sisters were horrified when I told them later how I saw Dad. They grew up in the same house as me, and found it hard to believe some of my harsh remarks of resentment towards our father. They had no such problem. He was their hero and they honoured him. They reassured me that my Dad really loved me. They saw the same events and circumstances differently, and that's OK. How it is, is how it is.

How I saw my father was how I saw him and, rightly or wrongly, **I made judgements based on 'poor little me'.** I'd always felt that he never cared about me or wanted to listen to me. So I just went on my pity-party way, looking everywhere for the pat on the head from other men. I got them, but that didn't build my father/son relationship.

In my 20s and 30s, things were better. Dad came to footy with me and we also had a close involvement in the harness racing (trots). **But we mucked it up in the critical time up to 15 years of age, and that's the time that can manufacture the problems.**

Clearing the garbage

It wasn't until much later in life that I asked my Creator to show me in my heart what life was like for my father through this time while I was growing up.

He showed me that there are always 3 sides to every story or situation – mine, the other person's (my Dad's) and God's. Don't believe everything you think! So if you are having a tough time with your mother or father, it could help to step back and consider what their side of the problem might look like.

If someone could have had a chat to me along these lines as I was growing up, I may have saved myself a lot of pain down in the deep and inner part of my spirit. I may not have dishonoured my father as much as I did.

I never got my father's side of the story because it wasn't the done thing. Dad did the work, Mum raised the children, and we were to be seen and not heard.

Even at 57 years of age, I still had to verbalise more issues that needed to be cleaned up. **I had to name them one-by-one and forgive my father.** Then I could get on with a new and cleaned-up heart and give him honour. I was no longer driven by the motivation of disagreeing with my father and not wanting to be anything like him. And 'all' started to really go well with me.

It's great. I am free to help and encourage my 3 sons in new and open ways and not hold onto any grudges, resentments, disappointments or judgements. I try to see things their way and not to have a 'sausage factory' mentality where I treat them all the same.

Today I am finally able to look at my father differently, and see the good in him which I learned to be grateful for. He was a very loyal man. He was a good provider and courageous protector. He loved my mother. As I've grown older I know that he instilled in me right from the beginning the importance of playing the game of life fairly and squarely.

What a shame we can get locked into mindsets about our fathers that don't show the whole picture. If we had someone to show us the other person's perspective, there might be a lot more harmony between fathers and sons.

Honouring your mother

I know a bloke who was born unwanted and rejected. **Even before he was born, his mother tried to abort him.** He was put in an infants' home. After two months his grandmother took him and raised him like a treasured son. At 12 years of age, he discovered the person he had thought was his older sister was in fact his mother. She had not acknowledged him as her son. He never got to know his father.

He went through life never feeling acceptable or good enough, never fitting in. He had trouble with relationships with women, used drugs to hide his pain, and ended up in prison.

If that was you, would you want to honour your mother?

This bloke met the Big Fella on a first name basis at the age of 50. **Over a couple of years that followed, he reached a point of forgiveness towards his mother and now has a good relationship with her.** He forgave her for the guilt and shame and rejection he had felt because of her behaviour.

He attributes this new-found relationship with his mother to his Creator, who always had a plan for him. He is onwards and upwards into the champion's place for the first time in his life. From a messed-up head and heart, he had the courage to trust the Big Fella and accept his freedom.

This bloke had every reason to dishonour his parents. Resentment and bitterness crippled his life until he got to know freedom. Now the 'all' is going well for him. You can have that freedom too, champion!

Understanding and forgiving your father and mother

So fellas, this gets down to you. It could be some little thing that happened a long time ago in your relationship with your father or your mother. **It has come back to bite you as a big monster, wrecking your present-day relationship with your woman or children.**

If you can, ask the Big Fella to point out any issues to you. **Write them down. See where you need to forgive and let go.** If it's too painful for you to do it alone, he will help you to forgive little by little, layer by layer. Remember that we said big things can take a while to forgive – you have to work at it. It will happen eventually, and you will emerge more real. You will enjoy the champion that is within you, and start to know that you are a champion son of the King.

You can still get there, no matter how bad you think it is.

Sometimes it will take many years to deal with and heal the pain it has caused you. You can deal with it little by little, slowly as needed. You'll still collect the prize at the finish. You can ask the Big Fella for help, and you can ask a trusted bloke to help you – if you don't know anyone who seems right, don't forget you can find a shed group at shednight.com.

Champions honour their father and mother, no matter what they've done in the past

What you have harboured and built up over years may take a little more time and effort to let go of. You won't regret the hard work when the 'all' starts to go well with you.

I took too long to learn this freedom in my life. I want to encourage you to look closely at your position, even though some of you will say, 'But my father or mother is dead and gone and I'm 50 or 60.'

Don't let the deceiver con you on that. **Your freedom can free up your woman, children and grandchildren.** You don't want them to carry any of your hang-ups.

You can do it. If you have come to a secure place with the Big Fella and are asking him to teach you to trust him more, then this one can be an amazing relief.

You get to drop off all this baggage about your father and mother that you didn't even know you'd carried. You'll feel like you'd been running the race with two bags of concrete on your shoulders, or you'd been dragging a truck tyre along with you everywhere you went. Now you can enjoy life in freedom and get to feel like a real-deal champion.

When 'all' goes well

As my Dad got closer to the end of his life, something great happened.

Earlier when I visited him, we always seemed to get into an argument over our different political views and I would leave all steamed-up. I would have a little meltdown on the way home and say that I wasn't going to visit him again.

We always ended up blueing and that wasn't how I wanted this time of our lives to end. He loved me and I loved him.

So! What about this? I gave up trying to say the right things and treading on broken eggshells. **I had a red-hot desperate talk to the Bloke Upstairs. I said I'd done my best and it wasn't working.** I wanted for Dad and me to hit it off, right through to the end.

And yes, I asked my Creator to do a job on the inside of me, so that I would be his man when I was with Dad.

After that, every visit started with a handshake (although I would have liked a hug or a hand around the shoulder, a handshake was a good start!). From that talk to the Big Fella, I let him take charge over my heart and spirit. **What came out of my mouth was God-motivated, not Ian-manipulated.**

The handshake got longer and longer, and we were talking and hearing each other from inside of our hearts.

I just had to 'let go and let God', and Dad and I got on like champions till the day he died. **I had to change so he could get close in to my heart.** It turned out champion for me.

Even though through my life the father/son thing was terrible sometimes, I lay on the bed and cried and cried like a little boy when he died. Dad and I had finally worked together on our relationship in the later years. He showed me how proud of me he was.

If you haven't got a father and you're saying, 'It's OK for you Watto', take heart, how about this? God said to his son Jesus, 'You are my boy and I'm well pleased with you.' **He wants to sit each of us on his knee and put his big arm around us and say, 'You are my boy and I'm well pleased with you.'**

Get a hold of this, grab it with both hands. To whatever degree 'all' is not going well in our lives, we've got to do something about honouring our father and mother. When we do, we find that 'all' becomes total freedom within.

In the meantime, look for a stand-in father. You'll find one that will love to encourage you along your journey.

How to be a father your children can honour

I heard a school chaplain asked the following question in front of 800+ blokes: 'After 16 years as chaplain to boys, girls, parents and teachers, what have you learned to pass onto us blokes?' He replied, '**Lots of the problems that girls and boys have go back to their fathers. It's not only what we did, but also the things we failed to do.**'

I am a father of 3 sons. It is vital for me to have a serious look at my relationship with my own father, and how that is affecting my relationship with my children. **I don't want to pass on any negatives to my sons.** I want them to be able to go into their adult lives with freedom from any of my hang-ups.

Get this 'honouring fathers and mothers' part right, and it gives you freedom in your own head, to help create more freedom in the heads and hearts of your children.

Through my life I've learned to try to love and encourage my boys as individuals just as they are. My wish is to continue to encourage them to **be who they are, and to know Whose they are.** They were the Creator's before they were mine. I take it as an honour and a privilege to have them in my life.

Don't get this bit wrong with your children. Tell them and show them how important they are to you. And show them how you honour your own parents.

It's so vital to communicate with your children. When they really are arcing-up about something that's happened between you, you can show them there's another side to the story. **Help them understand your side of the story.**

And think: what about your father or mother? How did they see things in their relationship with you? What was their side of the story?

With both your children and your parents, get a better conclusion instead of just living life in a narrow-minded way that hurts everyone.

And if your children are grown-up, you still have an amazing opportunity to sort this out by a letter saying you're sorry. You're never too old to learn and change and grow. If you **keep the communication open and alive**, it's marvellous how freeing it is for everyone.

The take-home message

The Big Fella can take you from years of hurt and pain into the champion's team.

Dishonouring your parents is like a cancer. It eats away inside you and you're not even aware of it. **Do your maintenance on this one.** If you don't have the checkups, one day you're going to find it blows up in your face and you've got a big battle you didn't need to have.

Sometimes you can say, 'Yes, I've got most of the issues sorted out with my parents.' Well, that's good, but don't settle for 'most'. Get it dealt with so it's done and dusted. It's worth getting it 'all' sorted so that 'all' goes well!

Don't get lost in the middlemen. **Go straight to the top and remind the Big Fella of this promise that if you honour your father and mother, 'all' will go well with you.**

Tell your Creator you want to take it up with no strings attached. And, you know, if you ask him to give you a few champions along the way to help you, he will do that too. He's done it for me all along the way of my life, and he's still doing it for me at 66.

If you do honour your father and your mother, you will feel like a million dollars. It helps me have my feet on the ground and be confident in who I am. You can have freedom too, champion!

TO REMEMBER…

'All' means all. I looked it up in the dictionary!

Get it sorted out with your parents so all goes well for you.

Honour the position, so you can deal with any wrongdoing.

We can drop the baggage that wrecks the inner part of our being and enjoy life in freedom.

Realise that there's 3 sides to every story.

Honour your parents, and be in the champion's team of freedom.

BONUS:

Some more gems from the *Work Manual*…

Children, you belong to the Lord, and you do the right thing when you obey your parents. The first commandment with a promise says, "**Obey your father and your mother, and you will have a long and happy life.**" Parents, don't be hard on your children. Raise them properly. Teach them and instruct them about the Lord. (Ephesians 6:1-4)

Respect your father and mother, and you will live a long and successful life in the land I am giving you. (Deuteronomy 5:16)

Champion!

7. Champions grow into trust

TO GET YOU STARTED

Do you ever lose sleep from worry? Have you put too much trust in people and been let down? Have you thought trust was a deal you had to make, a battle between two minds, with an underlying fear of getting dudded? Have you had trouble trusting authority?

Have you needed to get between a rock and a hard place to find out about trust?

Then welcome to parts of my journey. Let me encourage you out of and through these bumps in the road into the champion life, being able to trust and feel secure in who you are.

Life starts with trust

We do things every day that require trust. Think of how you have to trust that your brakes work in your car when you apply the pedal. You trust in the pilot when you buckle up for your plane flight. A visually impaired person has to trust their guide dog or their walking cane.

America coined the saying 'In God We Trust' – it's even on their money. Couldn't be any better than that. Do you think they all believe it and do it?! If trust had been that easy for me, gee, life would have been a lot cruisier.

Unwavering trust is a rare and a precious thing. It needs the courage of a champion to bring out the miracles of life that come from trust.

Afraid to trust

We are born knowing how to trust, because little babies have to trust their parents. They have no other way of survival. That's why it hurts the whole of society when an adult has broken the trust of a child who doesn't deserve it and can't do anything about it. That harmed child learns to stop trusting.

For many of us as we grow older, whether we were seriously harmed as a child or not, the world's ways teach us not to trust.

I grew to believe that trust was all about a deal, and whether the other bloke would hold up his part of the deal – a little battle of two minds, like a competition. My mistrusting moments helped develop my hard-core expectancy not to trust anything you hear or see until the person proves himself to you.

I lived with the expectancy that someone would try to get at me or rip me off. Being a bloke, I thought I had to get up earlier than the other bloke and be head smart. **I didn't want to take too many chances with people because I had a fear of getting dudded.** I couldn't see that trust was something deeper than my thoughts and actions.

I took aboard distrust of authority while doing my compulsory 2-year army training. Not all in authority were in the distrust club, but there were a couple who really sent my distrust indicator in the wrong direction. I had trouble trusting authority for a long time afterwards. Their word was not their word. I still battle if it resurfaces to this day, even though I thought I'd

Trust is like letting the pilot fly the plane

shed the layers of distrust and was free. I hate it when I see a misuse of authority.

Our political leadership can also damage our trust. Some politicians can publicly go against what they have promised without apologising for it. They just help us as a society to have less trust in the system we live under.

So looking back I had lots of mistrust. I developed a fear to trust. It was all about me and my brain. **I wasn't taught or encouraged to let go with my heart, or taught that trust comes from deep within the core of my big turbocharged ticker.**

How are you going with this one? **If you don't trust anybody you'll have to live like an island.** You'll spend all your time watching every which way, and get too consumed by it. You'll be spending too much time in an area you don't need to, so other areas of champion life get neglected.

Your start in life

Did you grow up in a protected part of life where you trusted all around you? If you did, you've probably got a greater start towards trusting. However, when someone close to you lets you down, it could hurt in a bigger way because you haven't been conditioned by the world's ways. But if you have grown up in a trusting, encouraging place, use that as a platform to be able, bit-by-bit, to trust first before you distrust someone.

But what if you grew up in the other family where right from Day 1 you couldn't trust a word? Mate, if you've been dealt this hard blow from the start, have a think **who is the bloke closest to you who you think you can trust and hang onto him for a while.** As you start to get a gut feeling that you're not going to get dudded by this bloke, then you can slowly develop a bit of trust. Be patient. **It's going to take time and a lot of good people around you. But you can get there!**

Knowing who to trust

I remember my mother and grandmother singing around the house: 'Trust and obey for there's no other way to be happy in Jesus, than to trust and obey.' I never forgot it, but I also never stopped long enough to really take in what they were singing. When they went out of my life, I still remembered the song, but I never got anyone to show me what to do with this thing that had an impression on me.

I let the world develop my understanding of trust and, wow, how wrong that was.

Because I hadn't been taught to trust with all my heart, I was left to determine trust in my head. I didn't see the logic in trusting in the Big Fella. I couldn't see, touch and hear him so how could I possibly put all my trust in him? I wasn't even sure he was for real for a lot of my early life.

If you're still not sure that God's for real, that's OK, don't hit the stop button, just hit 'pause' and take a breather. You can still make progress on the trust issue once you've gone through the process in your head and got the common sense of this chapter. This is a big area for men to deal with.

To learn to trust without the Big Fella, you have to **think about who are the most trusting and trusted blokes in your life.** It's in your good interests to go and chat to them, if they're still around, and ask them about trust. This can help you grow in trust.

Ultimately you're going to find that the deep, deep part of trust comes from the Creator of the universe who put the 'trust chip' into the core of you. That core only comes alive when you let go of control and say to the Big Fella: well, who are you, where are you, and can I trust you?

If I'd let the Big Fella teach me to trust him first and foremost, before I assessed the situations I encountered regarding trust, I would have had more sleep at night and less worry-nights. I wouldn't have got caught up in people's iffy agendas.

Trusting the Bloke Upstairs

I reckon being a true believer can be spelled in one word – **trust**. The *Work Manual* has this to say about trust: 'Trust in the Lord with all your heart, and do not rely on your own understanding' (Proverbs 3:5). Get that one going and you're on the money for a champion life, knowing who you are and Whose you are.

Trusting God not only in our heads, but also in our hearts – that's the full champion deal. If we only put our heads into it we will be unchanged, but if we put our hearts up, that will bring change in our trust for the better. **Trust is more than words. It's relational.**

It takes real guts and real courage to trust someone. Thank God he did a job on me. It continues today as I learn to let go and trust more.

The Big Fella doesn't let us down. Even though we may let him down. He ain't going to do a bad job on us. He makes us and he has a special plan for each of us, if we search him out for it. He cleans us from the inside out. He gets rid of the junk part of our life plan, and what emerges is the prosper plan, which goes like this: 'For I know the plans I have for you,' declares the Lord, '**plans to prosper you and not to harm you, plans to give you hope and a future**' (Jeremiah 29:11, NIV).

As we trust in our Creator – and that also includes trusting in his son Jesus the chippie – the **deceit of the world that hurts us in our core being is smashed**. We can emerge from brokenness and despair into the champion team.

What about you, champion?

So how are you going with trust? Are there a few things coming into your mind and you need to have a trusting chat to a trusted friend?

If it's deep, I urge you to ask the Creator of the universe whether or not he can help you clear it up, and help you to replace distrust with trust in him. If you are not at that place with him, you're going to have to talk to a trusted friend. That will help, even though with the Big Fella there's more and deeper and better.

It may take you time and hard work but hang in there. It's worth the battle. The victory is sweet.

Yes, people will let you down sometimes. You'll get a bit disappointed with me from time to time!

There was a man I'd placed on a high pedestal of trust when I was young. In my heart he was a hero. One day my trust in him was smashed. He expected me to accept and agree to recognise his long-time girlfriend, despite the fact that he was married. His wife was also someone I'd loved and respected for a long time.

Margaret gave me good advice to help me deal with this betrayal of trust. It goes like this: **Expect nothing from people and you'll never be disappointed.** Don't place unfair expectations on people, and don't believe all you think about other people.

I don't mean by that, that we expect everyone to fail us. We don't go into a situation expecting to get dudded so we can say, 'Gotcha!'. We respect trust.

But we **accept people for who they are.** Anything we get from them will be a bonus. It's been good for me and it works.

One of my closest mates and I have spent 45 years growing trust, through time and effort. Through many, many chats **our relationship has developed the top quality fruits of trust.** A trusting mateship can give us a glimpse of how much the champion trust will develop if the same amount of time and effort is spent with God. If I'd trusted God for the same 45 years, how much better for me in every situation! Don't wait as long as I did!

When you can trust your Creator's love you will be well and truly in the champion's team and be inspirational to those around you.

The big test

The last 9 years has been an interesting time for me in learning trust. We may think we're going great in our trust. We really get to know if that's true when we hit a fair-dinkum dry gully.

Prostate cancer was mine. I had the prostate gland removed and 5 years later I had 33 days of radiation. Then 2 years later, under the guidance of my radiologist and oncologist I'm now working with a naturopath.

I have to trust the medical people who give me their best to help me. I have no alternative. It's hard. Are they, the medical team, really taking me seriously? Do they get it right? Do they get it wrong?

You get to that space between a rock and a hard place and you have to learn trust. This chapter has become a little bit spiro, and certainly for me it has to be. Where I'm sitting, the question is: **is it just me, or is it me in the hands of my Creator.**

I'm happy to pass onto you that I'm very strong in trusting my Creator. So I hope you don't have to wait as long as I did to accept the challenge.

Out of all this I know I'm more real and am in a great place, because I've come to know, big-time, it's all about him – my Creator and Rescuer. I'm in his hands. Right smack bang in the hey-diddle-diddle of the palm of his hand. And I feel solid.

I ask God to teach me to trust him more in all things each day. It isn't about how much my beautiful wife loves me, or my family's support, or having a positive attitude, like society tells me it is. **It's all about trusting him and knowing Whose I am, that I'm safe with someone I can trust.**

> I know he blew breath into me
> at the start
> and only he
> will take me to eternity.

So I can charge on and enjoy the fantastic life he gives me to be the real-deal he created me to be. I know that I am Ian Frederick Hamilton Watson, champion son of the King. I want to encourage every other bloke he put in my life to know that he, too, is a champion son, just like I am.

Trusting the Healer

Some anxieties and depressions and other head pains that can torture us are helped to be cured by the clean and clear trust in the Creator. **He can free us on the inside, the deepest** deep part of the inside. He can also guide us to the best medical treatment if that's needed.

It's an extra dimension. These depressions and anxieties and other things can be helped in 2 ways: in the spiritual area that we don't know a lot about, but also in the medical field.

I've learned to trust the Number 1 Healer first and his medical staff second. Sadly, today's society gets this back to front. Society says world's way first, God somewhere else or nowhere. It's a bit of a worry when I look back over my years. I've done it mainly the world's way and it didn't set me up to be a trusting winner.

So I continue to be a work in progress because **my first reaction now is to trust**, and not to put the distrust-guard up. This is the healthy way to know I'm a champion son of the King.

A work in progress

At 57 I discovered 9 issues that I was still holding on to regarding dishonouring my father. He's been gone from this world now for quite a few years. Again, because I was getting to know my Creator bit-by-bit, I had the courage to trust him and I proceeded to sort it out. Nine years later, I know it worked.

It was just God and me in the middle of the night. I woke up and went to some study notes I'd been working on that were about forgiveness. I can show you today where I clearly wrote down 9 issues that I still hadn't really forgiven my father for. 'Come on Watto,' said the Big Fella, 'you can trust me!'

He asked me to call out each of those issues one at a time, and then to ask him to get the pressure cleaner out for me. He washed me up clean to **change my patterns and structures** to be free of these past issues – all scary trust issues for me.

Phew! I'm glad he never leaves me. **He knows when and how much I can handle, even when I might get the wobbles with him.**

I've been able to show what I wrote that night to many others having similar battles. I can thank only the Big Fella for this. I know it's different for each of us. He takes us right where we are and gives us what's best for us.

Dealing with the past

Some people will say that once you become a believer in Jesus, all the past is instantly dealt with. Because of this, someone once tried to talk me out of seeking inner healing of my mistrust issues. But God has me on a different journey. He continues to sort me out from the inside out and I am grateful.

With most of the stuff that I've had to face in my journey, my Creator has gently brought it to the fore in different parts of my life. I've had to look at it, confront it, thank him for showing me, clean it up and get on with it.

I'm not living in the past. I'm learning from the past and going forward.

Not everyone will see it the same way or have the same experience about learning to trust. Everyone is at a different place. **Don't discredit someone else or judge them.** But don't get lost at the starting blocks because someone else sees it differently to you.

Everyone is on a different course. Just go to the Top Bloke. That's my best advice.

The take-home message

You're never too late or too old to learn or change. But you've gotta wanna!

From time to time my Creator reveals to me more stuff that he wants me to hand over and let go of. As he's taught me to trust him more, each time he graciously makes me more like his boy Jesus.

If this trust chapter is helping you towards sorting out your stuff, great! Rip into it. Have a red-hot talk to the Big Fella. **Any previous dramas in your life about trust, he will help you drop into the ocean of no return.** He will put you on the freedom road into the champion team and you will know you are more the real-deal.

So today I encourage you, whatever stage you're at in life, he knows and he'll guide you through to the champion team.

Don't get waylaid by stuff or other people's ideas. Go straight to the Big Fella.

I keep my eyes on him and my heart open to him. I can't go back to my old ways.

He loves each one of us. He knows what's ticking in our head and our hearts. He knows what's best for us to learn trust.

TO REMEMBER...

Trust is golden. Trust is letting go.

Trust is:
faith
courage
peace within
comfort.

Trust may be:
taking a chance
scary.

Trust can be:
learned
experienced
taught and caught.

Trust becomes security... in who you are and Whose you are, belonging to your Creator.

BONUS:

The *Work Manual* contains some gems about trusting the Big Fella, each other, and even the government:

> With all your heart you must trust the Lord and not your own judgement. **Always let him lead you and he will clear the road for you to follow.** (Proverbs 3:5-6)

> The Lord is a mighty rock, and he never does wrong. **God can always be trusted to bring justice.** (Deuteronomy 32:4)

> **Just as iron sharpens iron, friends sharpen the minds of each other.** (Proverbs 27:17)

Takes guts and courage to trust!

8. Champions handle anger

TO GET YOU STARTED

The last time you were fair-dinkum angry, what pressed your buttons? Was it your pride and ego getting smashed? Or were you just jacked-off big-time?

Anger is a mighty powerful thing. It can rock your socks off and raise your blood pressure. Anger in a marriage can wreck relationships.

Have you got a safe outlet for your anger?

Anger is what comes out of men when they wont admit they've been hurt.

Have you experienced the good type of anger, that makes you change things for the better in this world?

Let's have a red-hot look at anger. More importantly, let's look at where it came from and how we can deal with it as champions.

I was bad tempered as a boy. I'd throw a tantrum playing cricket if I got bowled out first ball. If anyone laughed at me, I'd feel like I wanted to hit them with the bat. **I never 'walked' – I didn't want to hand over the bat.**

My father seemed to be always having to sort me out. Now I look back and thank him for each time he did it. If I'd been allowed to get away with it and allowed to run to Mum and get sooked-up, I would have been so selfish, a bad-tempered little creep. **Thanks, Dad, for teaching me team values and how to be a good sport.**

The anger problem

> Anger makes you a lonely person.
> By being angry you make a boundary around yourself.
> A no-go zone.
> 'Don't get too close!
> He's had a bad one last night!
> He's in a bad mood.'

When you're angry, you're a pain in the neck to work with. It affects your friends. You're not nice to be with.

In our busy day-to-day lives we don't get too much 'me time' to just let off steam without being challenged. So, when we're alone in the car and we think nobody knows us, do we let it out in a little road rage? Or do we get on the phone under a false name when no-one is around and abuse someone? Fellas, these are not happy ways to let out our anger, and they can come back to bite us, big-time.

What about our families? **How can your woman be all sexy and beautiful if you come home angry?** If you want love and romance and intimacy, do you really think the joy and beauty of that is going to be tagged onto anger? **Anger doesn't get anywhere near passion.**

Do your children walk around on tenterhooks because Dad's angry and they don't know why? It's probably nothing to do with the child, it's just because Dad has a crappy job or he's been let down or he's got no money. **Children can be traumatised by a father or mother's anger** – not knowing what to say or when to say it.

> If you're a young dad,
> do you realise that
> your children will be
> watching
> and learning
> everything from you?

Of course we all want our children to take the good points from us, but sadly they can also take up the not-so-good things about us, such as anger. As we age, we don't enjoy seeing our bad points in any of our children.

> Anger in our society is not nice.
> It's like battlefields,
> it's like tsunamis,
> it's like rough dirty sea.
> Someone usually cops it.

Those we love who are closest to us are the ones that cop it most because it's probably the easiest way to get rid of it.

We've gotta deal with this one fellas. We've gotta go hard at it.

Watto the angry footballer

I played football angry. I played out my frustrations in life.

Some of the poor coots that I played against thought I was a maniac, because I was going ballistic to beat them. They must have wondered why they copped me as an opponent!

There's a difference between playing hard and playing angry. A tough football player, playing tough, doesn't go beyond the boundaries of what's fair and reasonable. In today's game you wouldn't get away with the garbage we got up to in the 70s, to satisfy our anger!

A lot of my attitude on the field was because of deep-seated anger. I didn't ever think this at the time and certainly didn't have anyone to chat with about it.

It was stupid and crazy, but when I look back, I think taking out my anger on the football field at least saved someone close to me copping it. **Anger inside eventually finds its way to the surface.**

Watto the angry soldier

In my twentieth year I was conscripted into 2 years in the army, against my will. I was unfortunate enough to have my birthday drawn out of the hat. At the time I was playing A Grade footy and was soon to be married. Margaret was the best thing in my life. My ego was big. A good-looker loved me, and I was getting a kick in footy – then bam!

In the army for 2 years, I felt cheated and rorted by the system. Ranked soldiers were misusing their authority and verbally abusing poor me, and I couldn't do a thing about it. I liked an argument but there was no possibility of fighting back! **So I just bottled up my anger** after getting eyeballed and yelled at and called many unsavoury things. I felt like smashing 'em like I would have in footy.

On top of that, having to go to the battlefields of the Vietnam War was a distinct possibility. **I got even more angry! I didn't agree with the war.**

Watto, the angry son, husband and father

When my father married his new wife, even though he did it for all the right reasons, **I got angry to the point of mucking up my relationship with her, big-time.** I reckoned that my sisters and I were not only robbed of our own mother (who as I mentioned died when I was 15), but we had to put up with sharing our father with someone else. We didn't get a say in it.

The method I was given for dealing with it was: 'Get over it Ian, and stop being a sook.'

I just got more angry and it bottled up inside me. I was already angry before my father's new wife came on the scene. The new situation just brought out the worst in me.

These sorts of issues were never considered in my growing-up years. It mightn't have been a fair word to put on him but I saw my father as angry. It was probably more frustration, but I sensed it as deep anger. I thought, *Gee, I'd better be careful what I say. I couldn't ask him for a new pair of footy boots or anything.*

When I was 17 my father told me to accept a clerical job offer in the public service because that would be the best thing I could do for my future. In those days you disobeyed your father at your peril. Take it or else!

He thought the job would be good for me, a secure career, all that he missed out on. **He wanted the best for his only son, but I didn't see it his way.**

Between the ages of 17 and 39 I developed a deep-seated simmering anger as **I really got to hate my clerical job.** I tried to cope with my frustrations and anger by diverting myself with massive involvement outside working hours with football, committees and whatever else I could be part of. Is there any deep build-up of anger within you that bubbles up from time to time? If so, you'll know how I felt.

It is fortunate that we had 3 sons who shared my passion for football, so in my hours away from home we did at least spend a lot of time together!

My boys had to put up with my anger outbursts. They wouldn't have had a clue why the old man got angry and flew off the handle. As we all react to situations and experiences differently, so our boys have responded to my anger in different ways.

My wife Margaret put up with my anger about my work. **It's not nice for the woman who's trying to keep the house together and the family happy, and she's not real sure why her man she loves is rumbling with anger.**

Margaret has never been an angry person and she's been a help for me. Peaceful people can defuse you in a situation without too much fuss and bother.

> **Fellas, what we really want
> is the simple basic love of our woman,
> but we're hindering it
> because of the deep-seated anger
> inside us.**

So can you see that if something made you really angry when you were young and you didn't have anyone to help you sort it out, it re-occurs every time? **It builds up and you pay it out on whoever is in your vision.**

A new way of looking at things

Ah well. As I've grown older and looked back I say there's no such thing as a bad experience. **If it didn't kill me it had to be good for me,** as long as I didn't take things too seriously.

After I cleared my heart of my old anger, I could grow to love my stepmother. I enjoy seeing her now.

I'm also grateful for all the people skills I gained as a direct result of my 2 years' army service.

I found out as the 2 years rolled by that not all officers are bastards, and they don't have to be, to get you to attack the job at hand.

The Colonel of my corps was a thorough gentleman – but maybe that's because he trusted me to give him haircuts every 3 weeks! But he helped to grow me up from the inside and also showed me another side of the military. I had some glimpses of how to become a champion over anger. I could see that a soldier had to react when called, and not resist like I did.

At our driver training centre we also train new instructors. My usual encouragement to them goes like this: '**Make sure that you start the day with a nice big, sweet, juicy navel orange – to make you sweet.** Don't eat sour lemons – they give you a twisted-up look on your face like you've taken angry pills. Stay sweet, happy and encouraging with your students.' And this attitude doesn't just work with students learning to drive. Stay sweet, happy and encouraging with everyone you meet, and you'll be able to become more the real-deal.

Good anger and bad anger

Jesus the Champion of champions got angry, not for himself but because his Father's place of prayer and worship was being misused as a shopping centre. He threw around the tables one day and drove everybody out of there.

Another time he had a go at the religious blokes who were making it hard for ordinary people to meet the Big Fella. This is what he said to them: 'You Pharisees and teachers are in for trouble! You're nothing but show-offs. You're like tombs that have been whitewashed. On the outside they are beautiful, but inside they are full of bones and filth. That's what you are like. Outside you look good, but inside you are evil and only pretend to be good' (Matthew 23:27-28).

He showed that sometimes it is right to be angry. **If it's good enough for Jesus, it's good enough for me** because the way he does life is how we want to get it happening in our own lives.

The *Work Manual* has another great moment in the book called Ephesians and it goes like this: 'Don't get so angry that you sin. Don't go to bed angry and don't give the devil a chance.' You've heard the saying: **Don't let the sun go down on your anger. Sort it out or it will eat you out.**

So anger is definitely in the *Work Manual*, and how and when and where it started, and how and when it is dealt with in the best way for everyone.

How do we know when we're angry for the right reasons? One sergeant really made me angry big-time when he tried (and failed) to involve me in an unhealthy sexual encounter. I felt helpless at the time to stop others doing what he wanted. My anger built up to become hatred and total disrespect that I hid in my heart for a dozen years.

It was 'righteous' anger at first because what he wanted me to do was wrong. But it was also loaded, because I didn't want to be in the army in the first place, and then I let it grow into something negative in my life. My anger from this event was not helping me to become the true champion over anger.

It took me a lot of sorting out to become the real-deal in this area. 'Stuff' held me back. However it certainly has helped me later in life to be able to help encourage others who have encountered similar battles to gaining freedom from anger. So if you're starting to relate to any of my journey, then the champion within you is starting to rumble.

It's OK to get angry! It's how we sort out the stuff that comes out to bite from time to time that's the battle.

The turning point for me

The turning point in my life came after hearing some **'inner healing' stories** from people who had travelled the same road, and from putting that teaching into practice with my issues.

The champion in me eventually showed and I realised that I didn't get angry so much any more. I may get jacked off and have a bit of a rant-and-rave to let of a bit of steam, but it doesn't come from deep down in my heart.

That's good for me and everyone around me. **Other people can hear my passion and pain in moments of disgust and not be shattered**, but I can give comfort and empathy to others where needed by telling my stories about anger.

So from hearing good counsel I could then take my own action to see anger leave my heart.

What about you?

8. CHAMPIONS HANDLE ANGER

The problem of getting angry is really not the test. It's how you deal with the anger. That's the test.

You're not going to get too far in the champion's team if you're constantly angry.

> The more you know the Big Fella
> on a first name basis
> the more you learn deep, deep trust
> and the less and less your heart gets screwed up
> with rage and anger.
> And the more you know how to live free
> like the real-deal champion you were created to be.

There's no such thing as a half-hearted champion. We get to know that we want to deal with the issue of anger. We can be more real, and at peace within ourselves, to do the journey of life. We may have started our journey with many **battles and bumps of anger in the road** – imposed on us or accumulated by us. But that doesn't stop us in the run-down to the finish line, sorting all the junk.

I jumped to too many conclusions growing up, and got all steamed up about stuff and people. But once I got to see where it all started in my heart, and I could get it out of my new heart, **things started to change for me.**

My anger was held in most of the time, but then something or somebody would trigger me off. I'd get pretty angry with whoever or whatever was in my face at that time.

Your anger comes out showing what you most care about. Most times it's about ourselves – someone or something has really hurt us.

Just think how much unresolved anger simmers today! I discovered this deep unresolved anger in myself. How are you going today? **Anger definitely comes deep from within the heart and we need to dig into it**, to see what turned it on so our hearts can be open and free. Lots of road rage and tantrums (minor and major), are a release of anger that's been simmering.

Once again, **anger is not the real problem. It's what you do with it and how you deal with it.**

Anger burns

Anger is like fire. When it's little like the flame on a candle, it doesn't worry anyone. But if that flame isn't controlled, it can turn into a bushfire that causes tragedy and loss for many people.

Anger is that deep, deep emotion that grows and simmers. It gets hard to keep the lid on it, and it eventually bubbles up. It can blow the top off the pot if it isn't attended to.

Putting cold water on anger only slows the fire down for a while. We need to pull the big burning logs of anger apart so they can be isolated from the main fire and the heat can be dispersed.

We need to keep a good close watch on fire, watching the winds and its intensity, and we can't be happy until it's completely out. Then the destruction all around has to be dealt with. **Buildings can be rebuilt after a bushfire, but people's hearts might be smashed forever.** The same goes for anger, because it's born and dies in the heart. We need to protect our hearts from anger – deal with it as it tries to enter our hearts, and guard our hearts.

If there's an angry fire in your heart, pull out the angry logs carefully and smash them up so they can't reignite.

The take-home message

Anger isn't always wrong, but we have to suss out the cause of our anger. **The self-centred stuff that kills and robs us needs to be dealt with.** Stand firm, dig deep. No pain, no gain!

Anger is a good sign that we are alive. But it can totally consume our energy, or be used as a tool to avoid dealing with a painful past. Anger can keep us from getting to the bottom of what rocks our boat.

If we suppress our anger, we may be using that to control others through guilt and fear. If we don't deal with the cause of our anger we can turn into haters. It's very hard to forgive if we are suppressing anger.

The good and healthy anger is when we stand for what's right. We want to right wrongs when something wrong or unjust is happening to others. Are you standing up for something that is right? That's OK. Stand for what you stand for.

Don't let the sun go down upon your anger. Sort it out before you go to bed tonight. There's a beautiful bit of reality! Come on! Sort your crap out before you go to bed. Does what you're angry about really, really matter?

One more piece of advice from the *Work Manual*: So be quick to listen, slow to speak and slow to become angry, because when you are angry you can't do life the way that pleases the King of kings (James 1:19-20).

The game ain't over till it's over. So let's continue to step up to the plate so we can do our best in all areas of life. We can get into the champion's zone when anger is in its right place.

TO REMEMBER...

Anger is that deep, deep emotion that grows and simmers.

It is hard to keep the lid on it, and it eventually bubbles up. It can blow the top off the pot if it isn't attended to.

We need to make sure the people we love don't get burnt by our anger.

We can be angry for the right reasons or the wrong reasons.

Putting cold water on anger only slows the fire down for a while. We need to pull the big burning logs of anger apart.

Don't let the sun go down upon your anger!

BONUS:

Some more gems from the *Work Manual*:

Controlling your temper is better than being a hero who captures a city. (Proverbs 16:32)

Don't be stupid and believe all you hear; be smart and know where you are headed. Only a stupid fool is never cautious— so be extra careful and stay out of trouble. Fools have quick tempers, and no-one likes you if you can't be trusted. Stupidity leads to foolishness; be smart and learn. **It's smart to be patient, but it's stupid to lose your temper.** (Proverbs 14:15-18, 29)

Don't get so angry that you sin. **Don't go to bed angry and don't give the devil a chance.** Stop being bitter and angry and mad at others. Don't yell at one another or curse each other or ever be rude. Instead, be kind and merciful, and forgive others, just as God forgave you because of Christ. (Ephesians 4:26-27, 31-32)

A kind answer soothes angry feelings, but harsh words stir them up. (Proverbs 15:1)

9. Champions know and apply tough/directional love and gentle/nurture love when needed

TO GET YOU STARTED

Do you ever feel like you're walking around dead inside, because you don't know how to express love to other people?

Do you know how to give direction to someone else without making them afraid of you?
Have you ever had an honest hug from another bloke?
Have you believed the lie, 'Big boys don't cry'?

Champion love is both soft and gentle nurture, and tough and directional with 'spine' – backbone with courage.

Blokes, we need both kinds of love! Let's unlock the keys to this treasure.

Balancing the two types of love

Directional or tough love means to call the shots with 'spine' – from the head or from the heart.

Nurture or soft/gentle love means 'sit on my knee, my child, and let me put my arm around you and give you a hug'. It's mollycoddle, sooky, come-to-Mummy stuff. (It's not sexual.)

The champion bloke needs both loves.

> **Give yourself a little thinking time to take this aboard.**
> **Many of we men have not had this passed on or taught to us and everyone loses from this.**

Mate, you have within you the ability to be directional. You can be the boss, call the hard shots, solve the problems, ask someone to, 'Step up to the plate and toughen up princess'.

This type of love has been mainly done by the bloke as it's more natural for us and it's what has been passed down to us by our fathers and grandfathers.

But you also have within you the natural love and nurture. It's soft and gentle like a mother hen who puts all her chickens under her wings to keep them from harm and keep them warm, nearly smothering them.

Blokes, we also have this love within us. If you let go, you can do it, and everyone wins.

The older we are, the harder this can be for us blokes to get, because of what we were taught. **Are you still holding onto the 'big boys don't cry' lie, and thinking you have to take a spoonful of cement and toughen up?** It is holding us blokes out of being real, and who we were created to be. It's got nothing to do with our physical toughness!

Fellas, this is an absolute must-have, must-do – to hit the champion's way of a great life. When we get this one right, the consequences are all good.

The champion in you will emerge when you let go in your heart and get the balance of tough and gentle love. Yes, it's all about balance.

Male or female love?

This balance is for both males and females.

For too long, blokes were expected to be directional only, and the women were the ones expected to do the nurture.

But a lot of society now tolerates and applauds woman's pursuit of the leadership role. (And fellas, if you want to make a comment about a high-profile female, make sure it's relevant to the actual position and not about her looks or personality or her dress style.)

**But men are generally shy about pursuing the gentle mother part of love, because they don't want to be seen as wussy and effeminate. Sadly, we can be discouraged from balancing gentle and tough love.

Enough's enough! No way. It's a-changing all over the land!

Hold fast, we can sort this out. **It's time for balance both ways.** It's not so much about gender, male or female, it's how we do the stuff of life.

This is not about sexual love. **This is for blokes to make a tough call when needed and also be soft and gentle.**

> **Get over the expectancy for blokes to have to toughen up.**
> **Rubbish and rot!**
> **Big boys and little boys,**
> **in fact all men and boys,**
> **need to be able to freely laugh and cry,**
> **to make the hard call**
> **and to soften up.**

You'll still be able to put your head down and go for the 'hard ball get'. (If you're not a footy bloke, that means stepping up in a real tough part of the game when the stakes are high.)

Same for the girls. **Generally, women are more the natural nurturers, but they should also be able to freely make the big calls when required.**

Unbalanced love

Too much of either type of love in a bloke or girl is no good! We need balance, so those around us can be best served and enjoy being in our company much more.

In a relationship, **if the woman does all the directional stuff, the bloke usually goes opposite and becomes passive and inward.**

We all need well balanced soft/gentle and tough/directional love

When the bloke calls all the rules, everyone can be walking around in fear and trembling. Then children will run to the mother's nurture and protection, and they can get lopsided in who they are.

Too much of either love is like over-eating at a smorgasbord of desserts. You can get sick and may need to spew out the mess to be feeling well again, to get back to balance – gently, bently.

There's time, space and place for each to do both as required. **We need to talk this through with our women and support each other for champion results.** Get the good and healthy balance and you see a couple going great. Then it's like going out for the perfect meal. Super and beautifully balanced.

Too often mothers are given the gentle nurture stuff to deal with, and fathers the tough directional stuff. What if a boy doesn't have a dad – who does the man-to-man part? Does it become mother to son?

> **Boys,**
> **if you missed out on your dad,**
> **get alongside another bloke**
> **who's your dad's vintage**
> **and hang onto him**
> **– that's if you respect him –**
> **and he will give you encouragement.**

Too much of either of these loves in our young lives can create havoc, in sexual and/or relational problems. Too much of one or the other will force unnecessary pressures on future relationships and cause big dramas.

So if that's you, don't stress now you realise this. You can make way towards the champion within you and get balance. Is there someone in your life today who can help you with either need – for gentle or tough love?

If necessary, pursue good and healthy bloke counsel from a professional counsellor, preferably one who knows the Big Fella on a first-name basis. Men are usually scared of this, but there are some terrific blokes in this field. You ain't a nut if you have to go and talk about life! A good counsellor will walk you through the tough parts of your past and you can experience freedom.

My family

I grew up with a smother of kisses, cuddles and sooking from a matriarchal grandmother who gave me 'mother smother love' – I loved every bit of it! I had this lovey-dovey love from my mother until she died. **Then I didn't know how to fill my needs for that gentle mother/nurture love.** I even looked to my older sister to hold my hand and mother me.

My father was directional – I was scared of him most of the time. When I look back I don't know why because he never hurt me. He loved me, but he talked tough.

Of course I went for the nurture/gentle love as much as possible, up to the time when a boy leaves his mother and looks toward father or other males in his life. My father didn't give me the gentle stuff so **I got the message that he didn't like his only son, which wasn't true.**

Dad challenged me. I thought he was holding me back, keeping me out of the limelight. He never seemed to put his arm around me. I can't remember being on his knee much. He couldn't have told me why he acted like that.

My Dad was a good, hard-working man. I heard from other people how proud he was of me, but I didn't get to hear it from him. It just wasn't what blokes did in that generation. **He grew up only knowing he was expected to do all the tough love stuff.**

When I look back, I can see that he was trying to man me up to the hard and tough part of love and life. Dad was trying to encourage me to get a bit of spine, but I didn't know it at the time.

When I met my now-wife at 16, being a female I expected her to give me the gentle nurture love (I'm not talking about the sexual bit). I suppose I expected her to make up for the loss of this from my mother.

I dumped more onto Margaret than just learning to love her, and it wasn't healthy. I didn't intentionally set out to do it. We can impose these things on the ones we love to our detriment.

Fifty years on, we each handle both loves in a well-balanced manner. **I am a touchy-feely, heart bloke, but I have learned to call a hard directional shot**, to call a spade a spade.

Generally, tough leans to me and nurture to Margaret. But we get it together in both types of love and it's champion stuff.

Margaret has always been wonderful for gentle love – not sloppy mushy, but real deep love. She also has spine to make a decision, and she's always been able to stand for what she stands for. I promote her in her life and she promotes me in mine.

Get this right and you get the top shelf of this part of your real-deal champion life.

It's never too late to learn!

Fellas, this can be taught and caught – if you are teachable. You can learn this by watching. Keep your eyes on the people who do this well and copy them.

> Have a big long think about it,
>   and see when you were told
>   to switch off the gentle stuff.
>   It may take you back
>   to some time in your childhood,
>   and you may be still stuck there.
>   Deal with it.
>   Let that false idea go to the pits
>   and get on with it.

One of my mates who's in his 50s told me that, due to his built-up hurts and disappointments as a boy, **he'd cried only once in his life. How tough is that?** His heart cries now, but the tears aren't coming yet. If he continues to talk it out, eventually they will, in a healthy way.

Many, many old blokes get the nurture love going as they learn to let go inside. **They might need to let go of the need to be in control. There are a squillion young people craving healthy, clean and respectable nurture from a Grandpop.** Sadly, some men of past generations haven't known this well enough to pass it on. Are you at an age where you can help young men get this happening?

Don't let what went before you in your family hold you back. Place a peg in the sand and take charge from now on. Learn to change so everyone around you benefits, and your future generations can enjoy both tough and gentle love. This brings people and families more security, consistency and balance. Are you able to help someone – a son or daughter – by telling your story on how this is for you, so they can learn?

Fellas, I reckon boys learn to respect and love women from men, not women. Don't miss out on this one. **Boys need to see how much their dads love their mothers.**

Don't tell 'em, show 'em. Say loving, affirming words to your woman in earshot of your boys, or give her a gift, or do kind little acts of service around the home for her. Make a special effort that the boys see, like Dad taking Mum out for a special cup of coffee on her own. Let the boy see his Dad give his Mum a kiss or a cuddle (not sexual) unashamedly often.

Don't hold back from becoming the real-deal. Your balls won't drop off! You won't get a squeaky voice or the hairs won't drop off your chest. This is a champion little gem.

Keep tough love private

Too many people get bawled out in front of others. It just puts them down and they can't get up. You pretty well always know when you're wrong, and you know you need to get a blast. But you need to get it in a way that helps you become the real-deal, not in a way that cripples you.

If I want to say to any of the blokes that work for me, 'Gee you did a great job,' I try to say that publicly so that there are others in earshot. It embarrasses them but they need to hear it in public.

If someone's annoying me like crazy, if I say in front of others, 'Hey, why don't you wake up to yourself, you didn't do this or that, or you're running late,' it cripples them.

We need to hear praise in public and directional in private from those special to us – especially dads to sons!

The perfect balance

Jesus the chippie got the balance right in gentle nurture love and tough directional love. **His lifestyle is our perfect example to follow** to get this champion part right.

9. CHAMPIONS KNOW AND APPLY TOUGH LOVE AND GENTLE LOVE WHEN NEEDED

> Don't get conned by society which says
> that Jesus only nursed babies
> and carried lost lambs
> and wore a white gown
> with a very solemn look on his face.
>
> He led a strong group of businessmen and tradesmen.
> He stood up, with no apologies, to powerful people
> who were taking advantage of others.
> He was kind and gentle to people who were hurting.
> He did decision-making directional stuff
> and had   both spine
>   and gentle heart.
> Take it aboard.
> We can learn this from his lifestyle of perfect balance.

The twelve blokes that took up and followed him came from different walks of manhood. He didn't just pick 12 blokes that were all coming out of a sausage-factory mould. Some would have been more directional and others would have been more nurturing and together they showed different aspects of the champion team.

One of his team, Peter, let him down big-time. **Jesus didn't bawl him out in front of the team and he didn't get all sooky with him either.** He forgave him and made Peter face up to what he'd done so he could get rid of all the junk inside, and then showed him how to go forward into the champion team from there.

Another time when all the mob wanted to smash this girl up because she'd been caught red-handed doing something wrong, he showed the perfect love. **He forgave her and loved her**, but he didn't say, 'It's all right to stay doing what you're doing.' **He said, 'Go and do it differently.'**

If you've been on the wrong side of the balance of hard or gentle love, take hold. The Big Fella will give you the ability to do both loves, and keep the balance right for the man's different needs and circumstances.

Ask him to show you how you reacted to your upbringing in these areas. Look forward to allowing your Creator to take it on. You'll see amazing things as you let him change your heart so your head can easily make the adjustments. You can become the real-deal, heading along in the champions' team.

Ask the Creator of the universe to tell you clearly what you need help with so you can show balanced love.

Remember, if you're not sure if God is for real yet, this is still very real for you. Grab it and don't be shy. Start doing it.

The extra you get from the God-part for this is that it gets down into your soul. You get the spiritual dimension of it, which can't be manipulated in your head.

Man today has the ability to give both directional and gentle love and so does woman. It's your choice. Will you do same-old-same-old? **Choose champion** and become the one you were created to be and encourage others into becoming champions.

Don't get HDD!

Don't get caught suffering from HDD – hug deficiency disorder. **Hugs are healthy for blokes as well as girls and women.** Just give them in a manly, healthy manner. The gentle, nurture bit happens naturally when you win that grand final and you can't hold it back!

There's both nurture and directional love within you. Give where and when needed and learn to receive both.

Just because you're not a touchy-feely type, don't starve yourself of this very necessary nurture love. You may only need kind and gentle words of affirmation, a nice hand on the shoulder, a handshake.

If we don't get it, we are nurture-love starved. And that's like the fuel tank on our car. We can't run on empty. We need to top it up.

Little babies can die from no love, and so can we adults. We just walk around dead inside.

Giving directional love the right way

If you haven't known the right directional love and don't know how to give it, don't despair. **Try it! Call a direction from your heart and it will be heard and will be healthily received.** This can spur on someone to great things!

> You can kill another person's courage
> with words from your head
> and inflict fear,
> 　　　but a hard call　　from the heart
> 　　　will help give someone
> 　　　　　spine,
> 　　　　　courage and
> 　　　　　confidence.

For some blokes, we need a pat on the back and a kick up the bum at the same time to crank us up!

The take-home message

Often, **bubble-wrapping us with soft and sooky love doesn't really help.** We end up with a soft society of boys and men if we just downright neglect our responsibilities and go soft for the unhealthy reasons. Women want men to be men, not passive limp-wristed feminised yes-men. **Boys need to roll in the mud and get a taste of both loves** as much as possible, and girls and mothers need to let boys be boys.

Come on, don't spit it if you have big issues or hang-ups about your own earthly father and he didn't treat you like a champion, or you didn't have a father around. This is a moment for you to do something about it.

Find a good and trustworthy father type for yourself who can nurture you. Then you can begin to sort it out with the Champion of champions and get on with it. Start by knowing the Big Fella, the Bloke Upstairs – in fact, the Father of all.

So if you miss out, it's your choice. You're never too old to learn. The Creator didn't make junk and he knew you before you were born. And you can know him on a first-name basis.

Don't go it alone. Don't be an island.

When a man gets to take this chapter in, he can learn to exchange manly hugs and greetings like 'love ya mate', or 'love ya guts' – and it's certainly not sexual. I regularly say to my 3 sons and grandsons, 'I love you', and we exchange good and manly hugs.

A lot of blokes haven't looked at this issue in their life up to this point. They say, 'What's the use of doing this now? I've got by so far.' **Don't be conned by a society that says men can't do gentle love. There's more to life than that, and it's all win win win, especially for those in your close family.**

Mate, you will enjoy being you in a new and healthy way when you allow both parts of love to emerge from you – tough and gentle!

Love conquers all! All you need is love, da da da da daaaa.

Enjoy, champion!

TO REMEMBER...

Champion love is both gentle and tough.
Blokes and sheilas need both and it never gets rough.

> For joy in the champion's life, man is not an island. He don't have to do it alone.
>
> Give gentle love and praise in public and directional tough love in private.
>
> Keep the balance up and you'll see that balanced love conquers all!

BONUS:

In the *Work Manual*, Jesus showed both tough and gentle love:

> Jesus answered (the Pharisees): 'But you let people get by without helping their parents when they should ... Is this any way to show respect to your parents? **You ignore God's commands in order to follow your own teaching.** And you are nothing but show-offs!' (Matthew 15:3-7)

> As they came near the gate of the town, they saw people carrying out the body of a widow's only son ... **When the Lord saw the woman, he felt sorry for her and said, 'Don't cry!'** (Luke 7:12-13)

> **The Lord is merciful!** He is kind and patient, and his love never fails. (Psalm 103:8)

Get the balance!

10. Champions grow to know that love gives life and lust takes life

> **TO GET YOU STARTED**
>
> Have you discovered internet porn
> – and is it sucking the guts out of your life?
> Do the blokes at your work bring porn
> to the office or the job site?
> Are you plagued by guilt and shame
> about things that happened in the past?
> Do you just want to love a woman
> and be loved by a woman?
>
> Fellas, we can clean out the past and become
> the real-deal! Don't miss this one!

Sex is good!

Sex! What has been given to man and woman for the best has been turned around for lots of people by the media and our society. **They've made hard work of something given to us as an absolute natural.**

How's it going for you?

As I see myself in the last quarter of the journey on earth, I reckon I'm entitled to talk a little on sex – the real-deal stuff between a man and a woman who love each other. You know what I mean: the intimacy part, married under the Creator's way. It's the most desired thing for man in relationship to woman, so the earth would always have people.

The Big Fella made sex good!

I've done the journey myself and I know blokes who have also had their view of sex messed-up, right through to sexual addictions and abuse. Generally, they don't want to stay there – they want love! I have seen that if they want to, **they can be healed from any of the past sexual crap in their lives, and get on with being able to love and be loved.**

I can only report it as I've seen it, experienced some parts of it, and heard most of the other bits. I reckon my wife Margaret and I have really experienced the real-deal sex that our Creator meant for us to enjoy.

Like every other little treasure, it didn't just happen. You've got to discover it. No pain, no gain, but the victory is sweeter for the effort.

Love isn't lust

I had to be taken through the journey to discover that love was not lust. **What I picked up as a boy going into manhood and thought was love was actually lust.** I don't think I'd be Robinson Crusoe in this.

Have you come to a point of knowing the difference between love and lust? Where do you want to be in 5 years in this regard? What about 10 years? Do you want to know what true love is?

God made women so beautiful, so everything. Right from boyhood, a man is chasing a girl. When we have a narrow-minded view of what chasing a girl means, we don't see the real-deal. **If we're not taught about love early in our lives, then our attraction to females can be just visual and all about what a man wants**, driven by the within-drive.

Our society doesn't seem to know what real love is any more. We allow suggestive comments and scenes representing sexual intercourse all over our television, and we generally don't see sex as sacred.

> However, I had a couple of great mentors to help me discover the absolute gem of my life: love, not lust. I had two couples who
> showed me by their actions
> to each other
> that true love was spiritual
> and came deep from within,
> and gave them amazing connection.

There's lots more to the story. I hope I can encourage you to source this through to the champion's way. Have you got any great examples of love around you to learn from?

Lust sees a woman as something to be used; love wants the very best for her. **The spiritual connection in love by far makes up for anything we might get from the lust.**

You know, I've met many men and boys throughout my life, and **the bottom-line wish of men is to love a woman and be loved by a woman.** No, I don't mean lust a woman and be lusted by a woman. He wants love! I mean for the whole of a bloke's life.

Why are so many blokes love-starved? And why has this been made so hard by the world around us?

A lot of the journey of sex is again all about choices. Choices you make not the chances you take determine your destiny.

Lust takes and hinders a good lifelong love relationship. **Lust doesn't inject life into love.**

When I worked in an office, there were always blokes who brought porn to work and passed it around. They'd just throw it on your desk. Porn doesn't help us. It only helps the people who make it. There's a very minor group of people who make lots and lots of money out of exploiting something that supposedly thinks it's satisfying man. It doesn't take us to the point where we get what we're really seeking in our hearts.

'Love hurts', but lust hurts more!

For the thousands of blokes I have spoken to, listened to and connected with, **many are plagued by different guilts, shames, embarrassments and disappointments in their past.**

Some have been sexually abused when they were young. Some have abused others. Some received STDs from another and have passed this on. Some are mixed up in affairs. Some suffer sexual addiction. Many have grown up unloved and unwanted, born as a result of a one-night stand. And so on and so on – all different but with the same result – guilt.

So why have we got to this point? Let's take a stand and do something about it so sex can be reclaimed for the champion team. Promote love. **Turn off your screen if it ain't love. And if it takes your heart and soul off the one you love, she will probably know without you telling her about it.**

This question in the champion's life is for real. I hope we can get the good guts of sex and get on with a fabulous, deep, love relationship.

The journey from lust to love

'Love is of God' (1 John 4:7), so says the *Work Manual*. It's the verse Margaret picked for our wedding and because it's so short I never forgot it. It works for me, but I didn't know it when I first got it all those years ago! The Big Fella is the Maker and Giver of the gift of love, including sexual love.

There wouldn't be a bloke around who can't identify how beautiful the Creator made woman – looks, body, hair, skin, smell, touch. But how do we deal with lust for another woman?

I chose to ask the Big Fella to do a job on me. I got to truly trust him as the Giver of the good gift, who could help me forever.

I asked him to help me see Margaret as the most beautiful woman around, and that I could see other women with appreciation but not perve at or lust after them. **As I trusted my Creator, he took away stuff from the inside out, so I could be free for Margaret.** The same thing works for dealing with porn.

I'm glad I've made the journey from lust to love. **If we just continue to live in our painful past and don't deal with it, it's like dragging chains into good and healthy love relationships.**

Still plugged in to the past?

Sexual intercourse is supposed to be so good. And it is, for all the right reasons. But when both people aren't free and real and open, but are strung up by baggage and connection-of-parts encounters, past sexual encounters that went wrong, it just can't happen to the fullness of its worth.

Each previous sexual encounter is like having an electric power cord stuck into the power point.

10. CHAMPIONS GROW TO KNOW THAT LOVE GIVES LIFE AND LUST TAKES LIFE

I was talking to a young married man who heard from a woman he'd dated in the past. I said, **'Did you ever have sex with her?'** He said, **'Yeah.'** I said, **'You're still connected to her.** You have to turn the switch off.' He didn't believe me.

I said, 'What if she rings you up next week and the week after – what are you going to do? If you don't turn around and run away from that now, you're in trouble.'

When we have sex with a woman, even 'casual sex', it's like plugging into the power point and switching on. If we don't turn off the switches and unplug, we'll have all those leads still connected, and keep getting more and more of them.

Unplug all those old connections, or they can come back to hurt you big-time

We need to be unplugged and unswitched forever, or they remain on. One day somewhere when you're trying to have a healthy love relationship, the old leads that are still connected can kill the one you're trying to keep right. Believe me, this happens without trying. I've seen it happen to many blokes.

If you're not connected to the Big Fella at this stage, you're not going to be able to attack this problem at the deep spiritual level. So if you prefer to remain spiritually dead, you're going to have to do this in your head in the best way you can.

It's going to take a close group of blokes who will keep you accountable. Eyeball them and say, 'No I have thrown away that girl's phone number. I will never answer her calls again.'

But your thoughts can still go back to the sexual encounter you had with her while you're trying to love your own woman. **This love and lust thing is an absolute cancer. It needs total extraction and continual radiation.**

Ask your Creator to help you disconnect. Connect to the higher power.

Confess it out loud

Thirty years ago I went to a camp where Bill Subritsky from New Zealand was the key speaker. I still remember it! He let loose on the sexual area for men.

He told us loud and clear that sexual sins and lusts needed to be spoken out of our mouths – confessed and cleaned

out. He said that God would give each of us the time, place and person to deal with it.

I had a few things to sort out from different directions. It took all my courage to do so, but it worked. Freedom to love and be loved by the one I loved was the result.

So you may be in need of a good clean out! God will allow this to happen so you can love. You can get a clean slate, no judgement, to love fully.

Sometimes the old way is the best way

Society teaches lust for love and puts no relevance on marriage under God. If the world's way is so good, if it's right, then why are there so many disastrous relationship breakups? **Why so many dysfunctional, disjointed families, and children who don't have a clue who they're connected to?** Not acceptable to me!

The more I see of this supposedly new way with family relationships, the more I'm sure that the old way is the best way.

Why do we allow our young guns to keep heading down this road? You must be given both sides of the story to make up your own mind. The legal profession are the only winners in marriage settlements.

Looking into each other's eyes at a wedding ceremony and spending heaps on a big reception doesn't count one iota for a successful love-forever relationship at the end of the day.

Let your actions do the talking. Make sure your walk matches your talk. Love comes out of both your heart and your head. The love from your head is about choice and decision. It can become mechanical if it's not accompanied by love from the heart, which is generous and open.

Take care that your mind hasn't been lured away with wrong thoughts by a woman whose own life might be screwed up. Her spirit is desiring more, and your spirit is drawn to her spiritual needs. Choices or chances – get out, go to another job, get rid of her from your life or you'll find you can be drawn into her spirit. The consequences can be long-term deep pain.

Fellas, be aware of the consequences of being sucked in by a lustful woman. We need to get it into both our heads and our hearts. How's your head and heart space?

Guaranteed, if you are isolating yourself and don't have any strong blokes around you, it takes a superhuman effort to stay clean and free. We all need mates who keep us accountable, or perhaps to belong to a shed group where we are encouraged (see shednight.com for more information about shed groups close to you).

Shore up your head and heart space with the help of fellow champions, and do the same for them.

Lust gets to consume the forefront of our brains and the consequences are not in any way helpful for having a deep, loving, heart relationship. True love comes from the deepest part of our hearts and souls, and generates real quality relationship. It's a spiritual connection at the deepest level – real love.

Lust has no deep spiritual connection. **Most blokes I've ever met are at some part of the lust/love journey and deep down want to be loved.** So let's go together into this exciting part of manhood. Wherever you are with a love relationship, see if you can further discover the champion's way of life which offers the deepest spiritual love relationship.

Don't be afraid to have a red-hot talk to a trusted man. If you are at a point where you are getting to know the Bloke who created me but you're not sure if he created you, that's OK. Just put it on him to give you some answers or signs to direct you through the love/lust questions.

By the way, as I've got to know the Big Fella for real, the less I want or think I need to take on any porn. No way do I want to insult or offend my Creator. **He has changed my heart too much to go back to my old ways.** He did it for me, he surely will do it for you, with the perving and lusting and so on.

Tell your story

If couples who know and experience the genuine love of God don't tell our stories, then how are young couples going to get the other side of the story, to be able to consider the choices between love and lust?

Love lasts forever.

Lust gives you the wobbles and kills relationships.

I reckon they would choose love if they knew. So let's not rob young couples. Let's expose them to both choices. Speak out, men, of the fantastic stuff, of your fair dinkum love relationship, so young people can see whether it's worth signing up with someone for life.

Today there are registered training courses and cards and induction courses for just about everything that moves. On the two most important things, marriage and fatherhood, there are no such courses. How dumb are we? **Good, stable, loving families are the backbone of our society.**

Fellas, if there are no training courses with a diploma or certificate, how about we train and encourage each other. **Men sharpen men as iron sharpens iron** – that's the slogan for Shed Happens, the encouragement group for men. (It comes from the *Work Manual*.) From what I've seen, boys learn to love and respect women from men, not from women. We blokes need free hearts to teach our boys and show them how to love women.

Come on men. **Let's step up to the plate and show our boys how much we love their mothers – not lust their mothers.** Men, we need to put the same effort into this area as we would in training a boy to learn a skill. The *Work Manual* says: **'Train up a child in the way he should go and when he is old he will not depart from it'** (Proverbs 22:6). Lustful crap on our screens is not producing the good stuff! Fathers who look at porn are not training their boys in the champion way of life!

Try this. Think about when you have someone who marries you under God's way and you lie in the same bed – not sexual. **How good does it feel that a woman loves you enough to lie in the same bed as you?** Margaret has given me that privilege for 46 years. **Without even a slight touch, love magic radiates from one to another when hearts are open.**

How deep is the Father's love for us, to give us that pleasure! How many poor blokes never get the privilege because of loneliness and isolation and insecurities – not the champion-team stuff. Let's help and encourage one another.

The take-home message

I hear from men everywhere that deep down they want to truly love a woman and be loved by a woman. For me, the champion life in all sexual areas comes from the King of kings.

Do 'supposed' love on your own, under the guidance of grubs who exploit girls, children and people for money and gain. It wrecks your head and your heart, and leaves despair and disaster for many. It ain't love. It's lust.

We pay the price. The one we love the most can't come right into our inner being, because of the un-dealt-with wrong sexual encounters. They need to be burned out of the deepest core of our being.

Jesus, the Champion of champions, died to clean us of all past guilt and burdens and shame. Take up his solution and move on free to love. Give it and receive it.

Our Creator is the only way out, with no beg pardons or payback agendas. He allows us to really know how real he is, in making us the real-deal for the ultimate sexual intercourse with our wife under his blessing.

I don't want to get too technical on sex but I hope you get my drift here. Keep it simple stupid = KISS. Only have one spiritual-sexual connection from now on for the rest of your life, and be blessed out of your brain.

> ## TO REMEMBER…
>
> God made sex good, for the true love relationship of marriage.
>
> But it's been used and abused. Love has been replaced with lust by the robber of life.
>
> A small group of grubs have exploited sex so they can make money out of something that's a treasure.
>
> Unplug the old connections, and confess the gunk to another trusted bloke, and you'll move towards freedom in the champion life.
>
> Men just want to love and be loved. Take on the Big Fella's solution and move on free to love.

BONUS:

Gems from the *Work Manual* – yes, it talks about sex!

You should be faithful to your wife, just as you take water from your own well. And don't be like a stream from which just any woman may take a drink. **Save yourself for your wife and don't have sex with other women.** Be happy with the wife you married when you were young. She is beautiful and graceful, just like a deer; you should be attracted to her and stay deeply in love. (Proverbs 5:15-19)

Jesus said: You know the commandment which says, "Be faithful in marriage." But I tell you that **if you look at another woman and want her, you are already unfaithful in your thoughts.** (Matthew 5:27-28)

11. Champions can give it and receive it

> **TO GET YOU STARTED**
>
> Are you doing it tough? Is your car a bomb and you need to replace it but you can't afford it? Are you still dreaming of buying a motorhome or a boat but the interest rates are too high?
>
> Let's dream a bit!

Are you getting and giving enough money, stuff and things?

Imagine one day all the people got zapped off the face of the earth by a big bang and all the money ended up in one big heap, pow! Do you know who would own it?

Methinks the Creator of the universe – he'd have the lot! **If he created the world and all that's in it and there's no life left on earth, then it's his big heap of treasures.**

It would be no good for the animals and the trees, they couldn't eat it or grow from it, and they've got by without money up to now. So it probably would just stay there in a big heap.

So if the Big Fella really owns it all... **while we are here on this earth, we get the opportunity to handle some of his money.**

Some get more than others. So if you have this privilege and responsibility, what are you going to do with it? I say we should ask the Bloke who really owns it all how best we should use his silver and gold. He may have a better way for us to use it, and he may give us more if we are using it his way.

So fellas, let's get into ways that will help us find the successful keys to champion giving and getting!

Outgiving the Giver

For most men, when we think of giving, most likely we first think of money – the dosh, the doh ray me. The cash!

Well, what if you haven't got much or any money? You've probably heard the saying that God loves a cheerful giver. Are you cut out of that? Definitely not!

But if we haven't got it, how can we give it? We can sort that out. **Give the other things that are usually worth more than silver and gold.**

> Give
>> a kind word,
>> encouragement,
>> a glass of water,
>> a smile,
>> a hug,
>> a pat on the back.
>
> Give
>> good advice
>> or a listening ear.
>>
>> **Got it?**

We can't out-give the Giver of the good gifts. We can't out-give the Owner of all the silver and gold.

This is what the *Work Manual* has to say on the subject: 'Each of you must make up your own mind about how much to give. But don't feel sorry that you must give and don't feel that you are forced to give. **God loves people who love to give**' (2 Corinthians 9:7).

It's really champion stuff when you can give and the person doesn't know where it came from. We just make it happen and then get on with it.

Champions experience and know the joy of giving. And it's champion to be able to receive something with a simple 'thank you'. I always say it's made round to go round.

Learning to give

Giving is a two-way deal – the giver and the receiver. We become both on countless occasions. It keeps us balanced, helping us not to get carried away with our own importance.

Giving has freedom and champion written all over it, but the world's way of thinking doesn't see it quite this way. Our society often thinks it's more about taking.

In Chapter 2, I told you about a man who gave me the idea and the encouragement to become a truck-driving instructor. 23 years later, I've got 6 training trucks and a very successful driver training organisation.

That man didn't have to give me the time of day – let alone an idea and follow up help to change my future for the better amazingly! He went the extra mile, and put himself out to give to me. Nothing in it for him. All I had to do was receive it.

His little act of giving turned my life around with high gains in all directions.

It becomes easier for me to be stretched in giving, and to give more naturally, after having been given so much. I want to help you understand that **the champion within us emerges the more we come to know the true value of giving.**

Giving and receiving is taught and caught. Giving is contagious. If we are generous and joyful givers we can actually teach others to pass it on. Don't give up. Keep at it.

Don't tell others to give, show them how to, and the benefits from giving, and they'll catch on. If you meet someone for coffee and say, 'My shout, I'll pay', one day the other person will insist on shouting you a coffee. Then they're away forever into the freedom of giving.

When we realise how good it is to give, it becomes part of our lives. **If you want to learn to give, start small and expect nothing in return.** If the person wants to pay you back and you don't need it, tell them to pass it on.

Giving takes courage, and receiving thankfully gains us freedom in champion living.

Trying to make ends meet

It can be easy to worry, when it's hard to make ends meet. This is what Jesus the chippie said about it: 'Don't worry and ask yourselves, "Will we have anything to eat? Will we have anything to drink? Will we have any clothes to wear?" Only people who don't know God are always worrying about such things. Your Father in heaven knows that you need all of these. But more than anything else, put God's work first and do what he wants. Then the other things will be yours as well' (Matthew 6:31-33).

If we've grown up with nothing, lived with the poverty mentality, or we constantly heard, 'We can't afford it, we have no money, poor, poor, poor...' **it's pretty natural to want to hold on to everything we can get our hands on.**

'Ah, it's all right for you. You've got everything. What about poor me? I can't afford anything.' **It's a poor and lonely life if we think it's all about us,** and we are going to sit at home alone, guarding all our treasures and taking taking taking. Yuck!

Learning to receive

When I resigned from the comforts of my office job and was awaiting the settlement of buying my first truck, things came to a thud one day. **I needed a quick $3,000 cash to take me over this month of transition.** I had no job and no income so I had no credit rating, even though we owned our family home.

How humbling. No cashflow. That dented my ego.

I mentioned it in front of a young plumber mate, not thinking for one moment that he would be able to help me out of my dilemma. Something happened I could never forget.

My friend had a chat to his wife and they came to our rescue. They produced the $3,000 cash and gave it to me without condition other than love. This was a huge moment in my life.

They didn't preach to me about giving. They showed me, and that's the way for a man to learn. Initially I felt smashed in my pride and ego to have to admit that I was desperate and needed money from someone I'd only known for a short time.

We paid the money back quickly but the lesson was fantastic. It helped me in becoming a champion. It humbled me but

I have never forgotten this act of giving. Since then, I haven't had any problems passing on the giving gesture many times.

> **I needed to learn
> to receive
> so that I knew
> how to give.**

They also gave me a wall hanging that I told you about before. It's got a picture of a fantastic old shed in a paddock, with the wording along the bottom '**My God will supply all your need according to his riches in glory**' – another gem from the *Work Manual*.

I have lived by the words of this plaque to this day. I believe it and it has worked for me. Hope it helps you.

There have been times when money and possessions can be, and have been, my god. **I was conditioned growing up that man had to work hard, and acquire and stash up the cash.**

But later I learned to put the Creator first, knowing it's really all his. **That put money in its right place.**

Unless you are a 'robber' – and you'll eventually get caught! – **do it God's way and you'll make more and have peace in your head.**

Can you give away something you don't need or like anymore? That type of giving doesn't cause any pain. What if you had to give away your best shirt and kept the old one and had to wear it a bit longer? Could you give your seat at the footy to someone else without telling anyone about it? That's a challenge!

Give until your pocket aches, and the real-deal bloke you were created to be will emerge.

Creative giving

A couple of weeks ago I received a large white envelope in the mail and that was no surprise because my phone bill is so huge it comes in an envelope that size! (Yes, I like a bit of a chat!)

But this one was different. It was a letter and a certificate from the Australian of the Year Awards. Someone took the time and thought enough of me to actually nominate me for this award. It was an act of giving from that person.

When I sat down and thought about this, my mind, my spirit and my heart were overflowing with joy, excitement, humility – and a little embarrassment. **I had to receive the gift of giving, even though I didn't feel worthy of it and I didn't know who to thank.** To this day I haven't a clue who it was, and I may never know, but it doesn't matter, not one bit.

But what it has done for me is to see the big picture even more clearly and to expand my giving wherever possible. **It triggered me off to think: who could I nominate** for something nice without telling them? Does that idea prompt somebody else? Hopefully it does.

Fellas, don't limit your thinking about giving. It's much bigger than just money.

Praising a person in public and discussing any problem with a person in private is also a great act of giving. Both are empowering if given from the heart.

One Saturday night, good mates picked up Margaret and me for a surprise outing. They took us to the edge of the surf at a beautiful beach, set up a table, chairs, lit the candle for the table mood, cracked the cork and presented a four-course meal all prepared. They treated us like royalty.

That act of their giving has remained one of my highlights. I received a gift that was loaded with 'more' and 'wow'. Once again, it makes it easier for me to give and to pass it on to someone else.

Real-deal champions give

Giving really brings us into who we are when no-one is looking. It helps us become the real-deal bloke. Are you ready and able to accept the challenges? We can't out-give the Champion of the universe.

> **This is what Jesus the chippie had to say about it:**
> **'If you give to others,**
> **you will be given a full amount in return.**
> **It will be packed down,**
> **shaken together,**
> **and spilling over into your lap.**
> **The way you treat others**
> **is the way you will be treated' (Luke 6:38).**

You can't take it with you! Why should we get the privilege of receiving more if we are too stingy with it? **Give more where it is needed and receive more** – sowing and reaping, harvesting and planting. It's a promise.

The more we give the more comes back to us. See how important it is for us to be the real-deal with our feet firmly on the ground. The benefits of giving cruise us into the champion team.

Can you take this freedom step into champion giving and receiving? Have you got it? **Give first and then receive, not receive first and then give.**

Hear it again. Giving is not all about money.

When blokes give

One young champion drove one of my water trucks until he had to give up work due to illness. While he was recovering, he had no wages. Something good happened. One of our other workers offered his reliable old runabout for $600 to get some more money for an overseas trip.

I worked out a plan. I told the staff if they wanted to put in, we might be able to buy it for our mate to help him get around.

Two blokes each gave $50. Then I told another young bloke about the little gesture. **The next day he handed me $500 for the car** and said, 'Give it to him without conditions.'

What champions – all 3 givers! You should have seen the joy that the bloke experienced with that car he got for nothing.

When a young bloke heard that a student needed help to go to the Seminary, **he paid the student's fees for one whole year**. This bloke is free and a champion in this area of manhood. Keep it up champ. There are fantastic acts of kindness in giving.

Another mate of mine read in the local paper about a couple who had saved all their working lives to set up their retirement. They lost everything in a failed retirement investment plan. They even lost their home.

My mate and his wife contacted them and gave them free rent in one of their houses, no strings attached. They had known the couple for 20 years and **gave without fanfare**. These acts of giving go on day after day without any publicity.

Give until it hurts. You sure will see great things happen around you.

Most times the news is about killings, shootings, road accidents, weather and the NASDAQ. For me, I wish it was more good news (and sport of course!)

It's a pity we don't hear and see good news about acts of kindness in giving, each day on the television and radio, instead of all the doom and gloom. That would encourage us. It would grow us stronger in good. I'm sure it would help us give more.

There are 2 blokes who have given me the privilege of parking a B Double truck (2 trailers) in each of their properties for no money. Anyone who knows the size of a B Double trailer and knows the road rule conditions knows that's a huge favour to me.

They each gave me that privilege with a 'Yes, no worries' over the phone, sight unseen. No big deal – typical 'bloke'. Neither expected anything. Quiet achievers, no fanfare. Two blokes who blessed the brains out of me with their giving.

They help to extend me in my giving. It's easy for me to return their giving by training their men from time to time for their heavy vehicle licence without charge, and loaning them trailers.

This giving environment helped grow my giving heart. Another young businessman in the shed over the road from my shed needed some extra space for 6 months. It was easy for me to say, 'Bring your gear and store it in the back corner of my shed. No worries, no charge.'

Pass the giving of favour onto someone else who needs it.

Gifts keep on giving

Twenty years ago I felt on top of the world in my early business. One day I wanted to shout a cold drink for a mate, but he was in a hurry, so I gave him a $20 note and said, 'Here, buy yourself one.' He didn't get around to it, but he kept that $20 separate to his other money.

His boss was always talking about starting a fund to build a chapel at one of the local schools, but things were tight and the fund never got off the ground. So my mate decided to pass on the giving gesture from me, and give that little $20 note to start the chapel fund. A small thing, but it started something much bigger.

Today, students at that school stand in an amazing multi-million dollar chapel built to the glory of the Creator. **What a** champion act by my mate to move the little $20 into the start of something greater. From small things, big things grow.

As I mentioned in Chapter 1, 20 years ago I spoke to a group of schoolboys to encourage them in their future manhood. At the end of the talk, I was inspired to give a book to a young man. The book was *You can make a difference* by Tony Campolo.

Twenty years later I have had the pleasure of catching up with that man. He tells me he read that book and was moved to make a commitment to his Creator. **He has undertaken to live his life to encourage others into champion status.** Today he is the Principal at a Christian school with a thousand students, and continues to encourage many more.

He has helped to make a champion difference in the life of others. What a champion!

The giving of the book didn't seem much at the time, but 20 years later it had made a huge difference to him and lots of others. How do you think I felt to hear his story? I gave the book and forgot about it. How good is it to hear the results of some little act of giving you were part of a long time ago? Out of small things, big things happen.

My giving, the boy's receiving and his continued giving – that's how it works.

What about you, champion?

Think of those around you and consider their needs, not wants, and in what area you might be able to give them a blessing boost.

What about mowing their lawn, washing the house down, providing a meal, paying someone's school fees, making a payment on a car, fixing the fence, giving them a lift in your car or doing something with no thought of payback? Then everyone lifts into the champion's team.

Lots of times it only takes a little taste of giving and receiving to whet a bloke's appetite. Small impromptu acts of giving mean so much more than we usually realise, and from that comes the great saying: 'Little fish are sweet'.

There's plenty of opportunities of great giving when someone is in trouble. Someone only needs to take the initiative to stand up and say, 'We're going to pass the hat around to help this situation', and away we go.

We can also look for opportunities to give people something that lasts, to empower them to help themselves. Remember the saying: Give a man a fish and you feed him for a day, give him a fishing rod, and he can feed himself for the rest of his life.

The take-home message

Fellas, I'm passing on a winner that gets you into the champion team, turbocharged. It's made round to go round – pass it on.

Even when you think, 'I've got nothing to give' – don't just think of money and things. Think bigger, ask the Big Fella to make you a good and cheerful giver. Give encouragement! **I've never seen a bloke go backwards with encouragement.**

You most likely won't see your name in the news pages or winning the Australian of the Year for your giving. But the Champion of the givers will never back down from his promise. He loves you, a cheerful giver. **It frees you up from the inside out and he's got a picture of you on his fridge!**

Sometimes you will need help or a prod or a poke or a nudge in giving so you can get to become the real-deal. You can learn to handle the stretching when you make the gift that hurts or stretches you. No pain, no gain.

The easiest thing to give someone is time, like listening, extra time without charge, to encourage them.

I'm giving you a good tip with this one. It's a sure winner on becoming a champion. **Let it go!** Let it go!

TO REMEMBER...

Giving isn't all about the dosh.
Giving is great when they don't know where it's come from.
Giving is easier when you've learned to receive.
A generous and cheerful giver is loved by the biggest Giver.
Give a kind word. Give a listening ear. Give some free time.
Give a little. Give a lot. It comes back like a shot!
Give until it hurts. You'll reap the gain and forget the pain.
Giving and receiving have you in the champion team.

BONUS:

A few more gems from the *Work Manual* about money, stuff and things:

> By everything I did, I showed how you should work to help everyone who is weak. Remember that our Lord Jesus said, '**More blessings come from giving than from receiving.**' (Acts 20:35)

> **Caring for the poor is lending to the Lord**, and you will be well repaid. (Proverbs 11:24)

He loves a cheerful giver!

12. Hearts are trumps

> **TO GET YOU STARTED**
>
> How is your heart? Is it cosy and feeling warm and loved and satisfied? Has it been broken and bashed and smashed at some time? Have you had a talk to it lately, or have you got it tucked away from all harm and emotion? Do you always rely on your head to solve things, and if you can't justify something in your reasonably-thinking brain, you'll not take it any further?
>
> Don't move off this chapter until you've had a red-hot look at your heart!

Fellas, this is my favourite – the jackpot chapter! The heart and soul of the champion life.

Your heart, believe it or not, is where the real you emerges from. If we close off our hearts, speaking only from our thinking, and lacking emotion and feeling, we can come across as dull, boring, cold or mechanical.

By looking at our hearts, we can begin a new and exciting future.

> If you had to describe your own heart in one word other than OK, what would it be?
> Warm,
> broken,
> bleeding,
> bruised, strong,
> guarded, giving,
> open, cold,
> hard, shattered, empty,
> full, romantic,
> trusting, imprisoned,
> cheated, small,
> big, mistrusting,
> happy, jealous,
> a heart of stone?

If you care to draw **a line representing your life, you can form an interesting picture of your heart** and how it's been treated throughout your life. I've drawn one at the end of this chapter, and we'll talk about it again later. Let's consider a few challenges, deserved and undeserved, that we may have encountered on our life's journey.

The heart of a boy

Consider your heart when you were a baby and as a young child.

Did your parents want and love you and respond to your needs so that you kept your heart open? Did you grow up with lots of love and affection?

Or perhaps you were left to cry unattended, or sent to boarding school when young to toughen up, and you have feelings of rejection.

There are many situations in our young lives that can cause us to turn off our feelings and emotions, resulting in guarded hearts. We lock them away at a young age so we won't be hurt any more. We say, 'I'm not gonna cop this again.' Hearts can start to harden very early and we can build rocky walls around them for protection.

Rocks around a bloke's heart

As I said before, I grew up with a sad, smashed and grief-stricken heart, **after finding my mother dead on the floor with the washing machine on top of her. I can still see it now.** She was blue and the machine was still going.

At the time, we were living in Mt Isa in outback Queensland. I had a good life there, but this event changed everything in a moment. Three days later, we were on a plane back to Brisbane. I didn't even have a chance to say 'see you later' to my friends.

Everyone was worried about my father. No-one ever came and said, 'Ian, how are you?'

Back in Brisbane, I used to sit up the front at school, in line with the teacher's desk where not even the teacher could see my face. I would sit there and cry without tears. The whole year I was in absolute agony and no-one noticed.

I tried to protect myself from any further hits by closing up my heart, so no more pain could be added to what I was hiding within.

Through my life after that, I always overreacted to death and funerals. One day it all came to a head. I was having a meltdown about the unfairness of a young woman's death. A group of close friends who loved and cared about me found me sitting at the table being miserable and they asked me: 'What's the problem?'

I told them the terrible pictures I had in my head about the day my mother died, of her hand stuck on the side of the washing machine by the electrical current. **They challenged me to replace that memory with a picture of my mother's hand in the hand of God.**

They sat and prayed hard with me about it. I didn't feel anything at that moment, but later I realised that there had been healing. It had helped remove the rocks – huge boulders – around my heart.

I've continued to live keeping my heart open from that day. My heart was opened up for the new world, and I can smile now with a free heart. My Creator kept his promise to me in the *Work Manual*: '**I will give you a new heart and put a new spirit in you; I will remove from you your heart of stone and give you a heart of flesh**' (Ezekiel 36:26, NIV).

This promise is for you too. The Big Fella will remove the rocks from around your heart and replace it with a new heart, with the characteristics of Jesus the chippie – gentle, peaceful, kind, open and warm.

Can you believe that? A new heart! This has changed my life for the better in all ways.

Breaking the rocks around your heart

Imagine I'm the average bloke. My personality might be to love and give things to people. But if my heart is still all traumatised because of the pain in my early life, you can't get in. I probably don't even know that I'm like this, because man is conditioned to be tough and not to cry.

That hard and rocky heart is smashing men. It's stopping men in relationships. Children can't get into their fathers' hearts.

Quite often now, when I send a text to my sons I say I love them, but it felt strange at first. **Men, we've lived in our heads.**

If we don't work it out in our heads, we usually don't want anything to do with it. Once you get the power of the heart behind your head, life becomes so much more. And if you're ready to have your spirit come to life as well, wow!

How are you going with this heart chapter?

It's not easy to jump out of our heads and into our hearts, if we've been just doing the expected blokey thing, saying, 'If it can't be reasoned in my mind then I'll ditch it.'

If this is strange and all new to you, no worries. Don't rush it. Just check it out in your own life, and see where you go.

Have you ever been in a premiership team that has just won the flag, in that moment after the final siren? Can you remember a time when you won something big-time or were filled with pride about something you'd done? **When you explode with the best emotion ever, that's the heart in you!**

The champion heart is open

That's why this 'heart of a man' stuff is so vital. **That heartfull of joy and emotion is within you, and it's best if it comes out where required.** For too many generations men have been conditioned to keep the lid on all this soft, gooey stuff – as though it's only for females!

Our hearts can be feeling stuffed in one way or another because of things that happened in the past. We can even be blokes who know in our heads that God loves us, and we're acting like everything is fantastic on the outside, but we're in deep, deep pain on the inside.

You've heard the saying: he's a hard-hearted so-and-so. That's when a man doesn't automatically open and let others in. **That man is always guarded and so it becomes automatic to close or shut off his heart to others.**

He may even appear to be a heart person, but he can actually hide from reality and pretend, so as to cover up his stony, rocky heart. I've always been an open-heart person but I can control a situation in a conversation so that I don't give you an opportunity to come near my heart. I don't even know I'm doing it.

At the end of the day, if you take this approach you're being robbed of the real-deal you. You're closed.

People may detect that we're not being the real-deal. They won't always tell us. Sometimes they just drift away from us.

But if our hearts are open and free, we easily identify with and are drawn to other open-hearted people.

If you don't really know how to be open-hearted, I've noticed that most blokes can drop their guard with babies and connect with their innocence. **I find that being around babies is so good for my heart.** Their dependency and helplessness can touch our emotions and bring us to a good place in our hearts.

There's so much more when it comes from our hearts rather than just coming from our heads. Our heads always have to justify the outcome, but with a heart connection comes freedom to be a champion.

Learning about my father's love through a dog!

As a boy I had a beautiful golden collie dog named Laddie. He used to sit out on the road, waiting for me to come home. He slept on my bed. I loved that dog.

We moved to Mt Isa for my father's job when I was 13. We put a trailer on the back of the car with a cage for Laddie. It was a long, hot drive over dusty roads. When we got to Winton, we stopped to feed Laddie and talk to him.

Then we got to Kynuna another couple of hours away and stopped to check the dog. No dog. The cage had come open.

A car going the other way pulled up. When the people heard our story, they said they'd look out for my dog as they drove along, and call us in Mt Isa after they found him. What was my father going to do, on a long trip with 4 children in the car? He couldn't turn back to look for the dog. So he told me Laddie would be OK; these people would find him. And we kept going.

I waited and waited for the phone call, but we never heard anything from those people. The rest of the family got over it, but I'm an emotional bloke and I never got over it. **I broke my heart over that dog.**

I was telling the story about Laddie to schoolboys a couple of years ago. Suddenly, it was as though the Big Fella said to me, 'How come you had a dog with a pedigree? No-one in your neighbourhood could afford a dog with a pedigree. Your father was poor and he worked his guts out to buy you that dog.'

I started crying, it made me that emotional. I had been holding it against my father all my life, thinking he didn't care. I got to be an old man with my grandson before I realised the facts of the case. I thought to myself, '**Fathers, we cop it, no matter what we do. We can't go back and change it. You**

don't know whether you've been a good father until it's over anyway.'

I constantly tell men, you have no excuses. If your old man dudded you, that's probably just your opinion. You're not sure. You must ask the Big Fella. If you don't want to know, all you're going to have is this one-sided judgement on your father.

If we ask our Creator, 'What was going on in my old man's head?' we end up thinking, 'Oh gee, I never thought about that.'

Look at me: sucking up to my uncle who flies me to Sydney and showers me with blessings, and meanwhile my father's working his guts out for me. When I love my uncle more, how does my father feel?

Even my uncle didn't say to me, 'I haven't got any sons and I can fuss over you, but your father's the one.' He didn't intentionally draw me away from my Dad, but he also didn't put me on the right path, because blokes don't talk about the heart!

What about you, champion?

Blokes, contrary to what society has trained us, imposed upon us, or passed down to us such as 'toughen up princess', or 'take a spoonful of cement and toughen up' or 'big boys don't cry', **it's OK to have a red-hot look at your heart and see what hurts are in there.**

It's never too late because those around you will benefit greatly from your new and free and open heart. You won't go backwards.

Fellas, because we've covered up our hearts for so long we can be totally unaware of our hearts of stone. Our outer bloke remains so obviously loving, but nothing is happening in the heart department.

No man is exempt from this heart-to-heart issue. **This has been screwing up good men and relationships for too long.** We can do a complete 180° by going straight to the top. Ask the Big Fella to put his promise into you as soon as possible, and see things turn around.

Remember, what you have chained up for 20, 30 or 40 years might need to be gently and slowly peeled away, layer by layer, to reach the champion in you.

Dealing with your heart involves your 'spine, body, spirit and soul'. So when you get around to dealing with your heart it would be fairly natural not to tell anyone else, especially another bloke, because he most likely has been conditioned by manhood to toughen up too.

You may even try to deny yourself the new feelings in your heart because you have never before ventured out of your head. **Take it gently! You'll enjoy your new heart and so will everyone else around you.**

We blokes most times don't get off the merry-go-round of life or stop in the one place long enough to even hear the soft whispers from our hearts.

When hearts trump heads

Sometimes your Creator will need to offend your mind (head) to help you mend your heart. He offended my mind when I realised in my late 50s that I had been holding this judgement against my father for being a lousy coot when he didn't rescue my dog Laddie, only to realise that he worked his guts out to buy me a pet. The Big Fella woke me up.

Sometimes in our little pride moments, he challenges us within, and we have to go deeper. Sometimes the way he does it doesn't seem smart to us.

Like that day those people prayed for me and my Creator dealt with the rocks around my heart. He chose people to help me who I wouldn't have chosen. But they're the ones who were there for me.

The way you think you're going to sort out the problem isn't always the way it happens. An unexpected bloke might be the one who comes along. You're thinking, 'Oh no, what's he want?' but he turns out to be the right bloke for the job.

If you only talk from your head you can easily crush another's heart. Your words can come like a spear in the heart. But when you can talk from your heart, your head is new and you will empower other hearts with encouragement and life.

Hard words from the heart heal. Hard words from the head can kill people's dreams and smash their strength.

Mother Teresa said, 'The hunger for love is much more difficult to remove than the hunger for bread' (*Time* magazine,

1989.) **Fellas, the world – our wives, children and friends – is starved and deprived when men don't give their hearts. It's too cold!**

When we meet our Creator and talk to him about our hearts, we will be in touch with our spirits because we come spiritually alive. We will have more of a 'sense of right' within us when we allow God to cut the rocks from around our hearts. We can drop off some of the past stuff that hindered our progress.

Champions, if we choose to rely only on our intelligence for too much of the time, we can become too hard in our hearts. It gets down to: it's all about me being in head control. You

probably remember many times when your head ached because you were overloading the old cruet. Let it go!

Fellas, have a little bit of a think. If we keep our hearts blocked and chained up, it is hard for us to appreciate the blessings our Creator and our loved ones want for us.

If, on the other hand, we are in a good place with our hearts, we will have freedom to give out. We will be able to really appreciate and consider those who are in the tough heart place. If we've been there before, we can speak life and freedom into a hard, tough heart. We can get alongside them and love them into life, and this will be a great help in developing the champion within us.

You know, if we ask the Big Fella to honour his promise with the removal of the rocks from around our hearts, he won't do a bad job on our hearts. It will be better for us and those around us – never worse.

Tough times can make you better, not bitter, if you have an open heart.

Dirty areas of our past can drop off. We won't want to offend the Champion of champions who gives us the new and free heart. The new creation within us emerges.

A rocky heart isn't 'safe', it's lonely

Fellas, if you choose to keep your heart locked up you can be rebellious and cause yourself to be isolated from your closest loved ones and your Creator, even wondering whether you are a created miracle or not.

You may have difficulty in making friends, and be just for you and no-one else – isolated. I don't think too many blokes want that.

We really don't want to lock up our hearts, but it can happen. We can shut down our hearts towards someone if we don't get our way on an important issue.

When we are married, or in a relationship with a woman, **if both man and woman have open, free and clear hearts, then we will get the wow for each other in love.** It will be heart to heart.

If, however, you have gone into a relationship with a locked up heart and you only do love from your head, this chapter will be a revelation for you. It can give you a new beginning in the champion team for your relationship.

Do you know how to receive love?

My heart was in disaster mode between the ages of 15 to 24 years from the deaths of my mother and my sister. So my heart was smashed.

However, Margaret came into my life when I was 16 years old and that was like a beautiful ray of sunshine beaming into my smashed heart to give me a bit of balance. But the deep-seated pain in my heart was still there. Inwardly I was screaming, 'I'm never going to let anyone get close to my heart again. It's too painful and I don't want it smashed again.'

Fellow champions, **I showered love from my heart all over Margaret. But I didn't realise that I was holding her back, not allowing her heart to come right into mine.**

I sort of knew in my mind that we could be closer, but the deep pain held me back for many years, until I accepted God's promise to take away all the rocks and give me the fresh heart. I didn't drop my guard in my heart even for Margaret, and I wasn't even aware of it.

Margaret didn't have any major issues to break her heart growing up, so she was pretty free. She could come towards me, but because I had this wall I'd built up because of the pain and agony, I held back from her.

I got into my 50s and I still didn't know that I hadn't been totally open. I hadn't been healed enough in my heart, because I didn't get anyone to talk me through it and sort it out.

There are many wounded 'relationship-bearers'. People are trying to have relationships with each other, and they're innocently being smashed. This stuff is deep down in our hearts. Most of us didn't even deserve to accumulate it, but it's a fact.

Nothing to give, everything to receive

When I actually received into my heart was when I had nothing to give. I was helpless in a hospital bed.

It was after my prostate removal. I wasn't getting better. Normally it's 5 weeks and you're back to work, but not this little ducky. My specialist reckoned I was putting it on. He said, 'He is a bit emotional.'

I was in and out of hospital. One day, they brought me home with another catheter in and I said to Margaret, 'Come on, I've gotta beat this. This is all in the mind.' Next minute, Margaret's trying to pick me up off the floor.

The next thing I remember, I woke up in the hospital after they'd removed an appendix the size of a big, furry banana! They didn't notice I had appendicitis until it nearly burst!

I was lying in the ward after the operation with 3 drips feeding drugs into me. It was a Catholic hospital, and **I was looking at Jesus on the cross on the wall, and it was a moment for me.**

Here I was, the big hero, the big giver of all gifts to all my family and everybody. **But now I had to open my heart to receive. I couldn't give anything.**

For 3 days I didn't know if I was living or dying, I was that sick. Margaret was sitting there by the bed and I said, **'Gee you love me, you really love me.'**

She said, 'Of course I do, what are you talking about?'

I said, 'No, you **really** love me.' I finally got it.

I was so weak and helpless I had no resistance, no defence to keep my heart safely closed. I'd had this beautiful woman there all my life (and so often, women just wait for their men to change!). That was the moment. 57 years of age and I love her, and I love her, and I love her now, and I love her more.

No holding us back anymore. **Margaret's heart and my heart meet all the time and it's like an unbelievable power that goes between us.** We are more in tune in all things.

Sometimes, giving is a defence

I overreacted too much when my heart was hard, and I made it all one way. My heart could give but not receive. **I didn't take things right into the innermost place because of the deep-seated pain.** I'm generous. I gave. Giving's easier than receiving. I've got a natural gift of encouragement which means I just naturally give out. But I had to learn to receive.

I was robbed and I didn't know it, all those years I didn't know how to receive. Margaret's been the most wonderful, beautiful person, but there was even more once I realised how to receive.

Why is the world missing out on that? Because we complicate the beautiful good news of Jesus and go on with all this other stuff.

I didn't know about trusting the Big Fella. We go to church and we hear a lot of things, but No. 1 should be: **love the Lord your God with all your mind and all your heart.**

We all go through life thinking toughen up, toughen up. **But if we actually deal with the pain instead of ignoring it, we have the opportunity to overcome.**

Are you keeping your heart hard?

Think of the times your woman has embraced you, prepared lovely meals for you, kept herself fresh and stunning for you, and given her body to you – but your hard heart has held her at bay. She's wanted to cry on your shoulder and let her defences right down for you, but she can't get in.

She wants to help you but you have held her back and not met her heart's needs, and you know it. She can't get sexually satisfied – because you can unknowingly keep her at bay with your mind-play and not mean to.

Men and women can unknowingly defeat each other with closed and hard hearts, and wonder why they can't make it work.

We blokes can be imprisoned in our hearts. This is what holds so many wonderful men and boys back from being the real-deal champion they were created to be. But we don't have to live with that anymore. God's promise is a guaranteed 'get out of jail card'.

Enough's enough! **Don't be conned and starved for true, deep love and intimacy from the one who loves you, because of your locked-up ticker.**

Listen to your heart

You may be starting to see why it's easy to be drawn and attracted to heart people. Others you don't want a bar of, because they are as hard as nails. Lots of what goes on in your heart is not a matter of words. Heart beams out of your being.

We blokes can refuse to respond to the signals our minds get from our hearts. Usually we'll just get busier and keep operating only in our heads. We can lock it away and refuse to deal with it. We can even deny the pain and talk tough, as a camouflage.

Your heart will discern things your mind cannot fathom, and your heart will remember many things that we try to forget. It all starts in our hearts – pain, aches, sex, fatigue, hunger, rage, anger, ecstasy and fear to name a few.

So we are hobbled if we refuse to deal with it. Come on! You can do it! You can get to the champion's heart.

Think about a breakdown in what was once a love relationship that started in 2 hearts. One partner makes a choice to lock down their heart, and the relationship is immediately in big trouble. Sometimes one can't take the tough and hardened heart of the other anymore, and it's soon all over.

Unless one partner has the heart to forgive, and give the other time to renew their heart, it will fall over. Help for your heart from the King of all hearts will give both your head and mind new hope and vision to get back together.

On your own without spiritual help it's like the boy with the big full barrow pushing it up a steep hill. He's got a job in front of him. If you think you can just change your mind and sort it out you'll go a long way towards 'hitting the money', but there's still that spiritual bit that you can't manipulate.

If on the other hand, a hard heart doesn't want a change of heart, it's over Red Rover. You've gotta wanna!

But when we use both the head and the heart, powered by an alive spirit, we have balance. Add the hands and the feet, and we're ready to serve in the Creator's world. Let's get off our bums and get moving, fellas!

What about you, champion?

I've had the pleasure of listening to many women tell me that, now that their men have changed hearts, everything is better. How good is that?

Sit down and have a red-hot crack at your heart and the Big Fella's promise. Weigh it all up. We'd have to have rocks for brains if we wanted to keep the heart all locked tightly away. **If you're a father or a grandfather, surely you don't want to starve your children and grandchildren of all that love in your heart!**

I want to be like Margaret's father. He had little education or wealth, but he had the respect of each grandchild. Granddad Ted showed them love and respect and treated them like they were good human beings.

Money cannot buy the investment of a grandfather into the lives of his grandchildren. And it doesn't cost money. It costs you just being you, being the real-deal.

My grandson knows that he's OK. I call him champion and I say, 'I love you.' He looks me in the eyes and says, 'I love you Pop.'

How's your heart-line?

Dig back across your years like I have on my heart-line (see p214 – yes, I know the text is tiny, but if you get the binoculars out, I hope it will at least give you the idea!). Write all the positives for your heart on the top of the line, and all the negatives under the line. Add words that best describe those moments in your life - good, bad, happy and sad.

That will give you the key to when things happened that affected your heart, and what age you were. Then you can see how it might have affected the next part of your life. It can help you work out what's needed to attack it, and get it sorted out.

Your Creator will reveal those moments to you, and who you affected, or who affected you, the good and the bad. He will uphold his promise to replace the rocks around your heart with a new and clean heart and wow, you will see a new and exciting life. You will truly know the real-deal in your love. **You'll never again want to go back to a hard heart.**

The take-home message

This is not rocket science. From travelling wide and far across our wonderful Australia, I see good and solid, strong-of-character men allowing their Creator to take the rocks from around their hearts. Then they see great and wonderful things happening for all concerned, and champions emerging everywhere.

Champions, I've enjoyed my 66 years and I know this is one of the best things to pass on to my fellow champions of all ages.

Nothing changes if nothing changes. Turn your frown upside down and get on with it!

So what about it? **I'm never too old to learn and change so what about you?** How good if we blokes can all help and encourage each other to get this one going great within us. It's win/win.

Well done, Brave Heart! You are now All Heart and a true champion!

TO REMEMBER...

Hearts are trumps.

God gives you a new heart.

Broken hearts can be restored.

A loving and open heart gives you freedom.

Don't hold your heart back.

The world needs and deserves men's hearts.

Become a brave heart and you will be all heart!

BONUS:

More gems from the *Work Manual*:

The Lord our God is the only true God! So **love the Lord your God with all your heart, soul, and strength.** (Deuteronomy 6:4-5)

You have looked deep into my heart, Lord, and you know all about me. (Psalm 139:1)

My prayer is that light will flood your hearts and that you will understand the hope that was given to you when God chose you. (Ephesians 1:18)

Hearts are trumps!

EVERY BLOKE'S A CHAMPION... EVEN YOU!

WATTO'S HEART-LINE

AGE	0	13	15	17	21	30	33	35	45	55	57	66
ABOVE THE LINE: STRONG, WARM, LOVED, WANTED, FUZZY, HAPPY, OPEN	Loved & wanted by my family			Met Margaret: 'the best' heart bubbles	Engaged & married: the best love	Birth of sons Haydn, Brendan & Luke: joyful excited loving / Trotting: excited satisfied adventuresome	Footy coaching U17 Qld 10 years: enjoyable heart satisfied fulfilled	Own business: successful happy & healthy satisfied challenged adventure	Church life: slowly learnt the promises for removing rocks from my heart / Shed Happens: healthy, fulfilled heart big picture of God joyful reality accepted	No longer driven to be opposite to my father peaceful satisfied	Ian in hospital: "Margaret, you really love me!" / Unlocked heart great & free	A truly transformed heart with no rocks: free happy giving receiving strong satisfied nurturing / Medical situation: solid strong trusting
BELOW THE LINE: SAD, BROKEN, BRUISED, SMASHED, BLEEDING, CLOSED		Lost Laddie the collie dog: broken heart	Mum's death: smashed abandoned broken sad lonely wrecked locked	Father remarried: cheated angry betrayed disappointed let down starved abandoned bitter vengeful (now accepting)	National service: cheated angry let down rocks around heart isolated very sad robbed / Sister Rhonda's death: broken devastated sad shattered shocked		Desk job: a loser's heart despondent bored unfulfilled disappointed unchallenged	Church life: mainly in my head on the outside cold heart not personal restricted unchallenged bound	A few disappointments with people in business: disappointed let down sad guarded	Persistent attack on business by one person: sad anxious disappointed guarded	Son Luke leaves business after 12 years working with me: good for him to follow his dreams but sad / Prostate cancer: shock anxious fear	

SMASH TIME — Gathering rocks around my heart

FREEING — Getting rid of the rocks

214

Champions become the real-deal bloke for all occasions

I've had a great life!

No matter how hard it gets, no matter where the bumps in the road come from, I've still got the sense within me that every minute of every day is so great and precious.

I only want to spend as much time sleeping as absolutely necessary because there's too much in life to enjoy! And it's not about money or position or talent, it's about who I am.

These chapters in this book are some of the major things that I've discovered. When I've been able to accept a challenge, it can take me into a really wonderful place.

Along the way I've survived and eventually enjoyed every fork in the road. I've had opportunities to take chances and make choices, and through that I've come to know that there was always more to being who I am and Whose I am – I belong to my Creator.

I hope that this book can help you at whatever fork or bump in the road you are at. Maybe it can help you have a serious look at something from the past.

I hope you get the opportunity to meet your Creator on a first-name basis. It definitely puts the turbo on the fabulous heart that's been put in each of us, and the treasures unfold. Ask him if he's for real or not. Nobody proves God to anybody else. But if you're not at that point yet, you're still a champion.

Champions are encouraged by dream-makers

I've never seen a bloke go backwards with encouragement. So on the way to becoming the real-deal champion, we need as much fair-dinkum encouragement as possible. Hope you are enjoying receiving encouragement.

Being around encouraging people is the best place to be. Remember to invest first. **If you want encouragement, give plenty where you know you can.** 'Do not withhold good from those who deserve it, when it is in your power to act' (Proverbs 3:27 in the *Work Manual*). Guaranteed, you'll receive it back.

Don't listen to dream-takers – people who knock your thoughts to feed their own negativity. They are often jealous, non-achieving and so self-centred that they don't want anyone to look more prosperous than themselves. Steer clear of taking their negativity aboard.

Keep in touch with the dream-makers who don't need to pull your dreams down to make themselves feel good. Dream-makers will have a genuine interest in your future and promote you toward the champion you were created to become. They are great to be around.

Champions know the Big Fella is the master of all dreams

For many years I unknowingly put the Creator of the universe in a box and limited him. Hope you can avoid this! It's his world and I now know that no matter what my thoughts and ways on a particular matter may be, his ways and thoughts are higher – bigger and better than mine. It's a gem from the *Work Manual* that works for me. 'The Lord says: 'My thoughts and my ways are not like yours. Just as the heavens are higher than the earth, my thoughts and my ways are higher than yours.' (Isaiah 55:8-9)

He wants the best for us and it's all his business and his consequences. You can count on this fact. Just know Whose you are. Remember, don't just look at the dot on the page, look at the whole page. It's worth taking the extra time to have a big-picture look.

There's no such thing as a half-hearted champion. Give it your best. Your best is good enough. You can't do any better. As we become the real-deal, the better we attack and stick at the task. We get to know no other way of doing things.

You might feel imprisoned by your current situation, but look beyond that to the possibilities. We could focus on the things that are holding us back like prison bars, or we could look past them to the opportunities that are like stars in the sky. See the stars not the bars!

Our character becomes more champion because, when no-one is looking, we are who we are. **We are standing at peace with both feet firmly on the ground. We can be counted upon and our word is our word.** We are good to be with, and we're also content with our own company and space. Our character is solid and strong.

On the journey to champion we realise that there are battles and disappointments that we have accumulated over the past. These need to be named, resolved, spat out and conquered.

Champions claim their bloodlines

When we get to know the Big Fella on a first-name basis we can claim our spiritual bloodlines.

They go way back to a bloke named Abraham, who was the ancestor of Jesus. The Creator told Abraham, 'I will bless you and make your descendants into a great nation. You will become famous and be a blessing to others … **Everyone on earth will be blessed because of you**' (Genesis 12:2-3 in the *Work Manual*).

Another example of a spiritual champion was a bloke named David. You might have heard of him in the story about 'David and Goliath'. There was a war going on. One mob had this big hooah who was a freak, wanting to take them all on, and the other blokes were crapping themselves.

This little bloke called David had been left at home because he was too young, but he knew how to knock out a lion and a bear to protect his sheep. When he went to take some food and clothes to his brothers he heard this big giant of a man carrying on. He said to the king, 'I'll sort him out for you.'

Every bloke's a champion. Even you!

When they tried to give him all the paraphernalia to protect him he said, 'No, it'd get in the road.' He only needed one shot with a stone from his slingshot to take on this noisy bloke who was all talk and no action.

David knew his Creator on a first-name basis. This big bloke was offensive towards his Creator, so David could go and do the job, end of story. Moral of the story: it's not the size of the dog in the fight, **it's the size of the fight in the bloke who's connected to the Bloke with the power!**

Has your human bloodline had various battles and issues that are holding you back? If so, you need more help than your own head and mind can offer, to smash it out of your being. Link up to your spiritual bloodlines. They're mighty powerful.

Too spiro? Remember, if we were buying a racehorse, we'd surely go back to the pedigree. So take hold of your own pedigree. If your physical bloodline has some flaws, go to the spiritual bloodline. You will come up with the turbo strength to see you become the real-deal champion.

Champions don't get held back by stuff

Champion, the real-deal bloke doesn't get caught up in stuff. **Stuff is stuff.** It doesn't rattle us on the inside.

Sometimes we can feel like we've been living our lives like a dog on a chain, all tied up. We run to the end and jerk our neck when our chain runs out, and we operate in this held-back position. We've been hobbled.

We make plenty of noise, barking and using all our energy, but don't see much result. We can't get past that point. We have been restricted for so long we can't get out of the box.

When we live life in the champion team, **the King of champions unclips the chain – but we have to step out into new ground and go beyond the old boundaries.**

Some still only stop at the same spot even though the chain has been unclipped. Champions create new boundaries. Let's step over new hurdles and claim new freedom. You have the real-deal character now to become a champion bloke, if you're not already there.

David didn't put on the heavy armour when he took on the giant boofhead Goliath. He claimed his spiritual bloodlines and his Creator's power to conquer the giant. His size had little to do with it.

Do we live life loaded up with 'stuff' that we think protects us, like the heavy armour they wanted David to wear? Do we need to shed the heavy loads that just bog us down, that nearly strangle us or that we almost get lost in? Let's get some winning solutions that work for us, and let's share these little gems with other blokes. **Winners are grinners** who experience freedom in champion living.

You are unique – there's no-one else like you. You didn't get punched out of a sausage factory. You had a mother who gave you birth. **But the King breathed air into your lungs. He gave you the spiritual life within you.** Let it come alive. **You don't have to do life alone!** You are not an island.

Champions stand for something

Who or what am I trying to please? The real-deal you becomes satisfied as you pursue a right life. We begin to cruise and those around us will appreciate us for who we are, and they will comment about our 'presence'.

What is our security in the walk of a champion? Where or what is it? Are we trying to compete with someone or something? What and who do we stand for? Why do we do what we do? These answers we uncovered to give us freedom, and now we can encourage those around us in all areas of their life.

Champions, if we can have our security in Who we belong to, then we stand for what we stand for. Life is not a competition, and as champions we are very comfortable in who we are. You're well on the way to becoming the real-deal champion you were created to be. **The Creator didn't make you junk.** Name it and claim it! You are one of his champions.

Don't tell 'em, show 'em. I had to learn to let my yes be yes and my no be no. Does my walk match my talk? Yes, if I'm walking the champion's walk it surely will. I like to live by the following saying:

> **Yesterday is history.**
> **Tomorrow is God's mystery for everyone.**
> **Today is my champion day.**

Make today the best! It's your choice. Enjoy the people you meet. They will be the best and most important ones you meet. You don't have to go anywhere else. Make the most of today and enjoy those around you. You will be content, with true champion status. You will be the real-deal. Dinki-di.

No matter how hard your past battles may have been, your spiritual bloodlines can help you overcome the past. You can do it at any time. Will you choose to take it up? Or will you stay in the pain of past hurts, battles and disappointments? Will you pursue victory?

You are looking at the step towards the freedom of a champion. Take it and enjoy the new journey. The champion life is true happiness from the inside out and it lasts for the total journey of your life. You are who you are. Enjoy who you are.

Champions are turbocharged by a word

If you have come to know that the Creator of the universe does know you and loves you, one of his promises can give you a turbocharge anywhere, anytime. If you're still unsure, hang in there, he's not going anywhere that you can't call out to him at any time.

A great promise from the *Work Manual* is: 'Christ gives me the strength to face anything' (Philippians 4:13). **I, Watto, champion son of the King, can do all things through Jesus the bloke who gives me the spine to do them.** If you belong to the Big Fella, you can say that too, with your name in the space. How good is that?

This one instils worth in us without any fanfare, because we receive power from our Creator. This works for me. Hope it is good for you too, real-deal champion.

What are you naturally good at? Champion, why aren't you doing it?

Are you still being held back because you don't feel acceptable in your manhood? Have you ever had a fair-dinkum crack at it? Give a man a job that he's happy with and he never has to work again. Do what you like, but like what you do.

Maybe you can take a hard knock playing footy but if someone called you a girl, you'd buckle. Do you go inwards and passive and turn on the mute button? Have you been emotionally bullied or abused?

Do you wonder if other blokes really accept you as OK? A good bloke? Do you ever feel like the bloke no-one picks in the team, always the last one to be chosen, as though no-one knows what to do with you?

Ever felt like you are nothing or a nobody? Not sure where you fit in today's culture? Do you feel like I did in my first job – continually downcast? Can you win the heart of a woman? Can you clinch a deal?

Champions get rid of the junk

Now's the time to smash all the negative junk I have mentioned and any others that hold blokes down.

If you're battling with any of the above, take heart. Continue to pursue the champion in you. As we become the real-deal, our spiritual bloodline will ensure that we can name the battle, get in close to the Big Fella and get the weed-killer out (God's power, his Spirit, love and grace who can be in us) and hit the roots of the past problem.

Come out without the weight of the 2 or 10 bags of cement you've been carrying on your shoulders like the weight of the world. Then you can tackle the new freedom of being the real-deal.

You don't have to hate yourself. Learn to love yourself the champion's way. You're OK. You're a champion son of the King. He will see you through.

The challenge of being real isn't the test. The test is what you're going to do with the challenge of being real. **Life's battles don't always go to the biggest or the fastest man. But** sooner or later the man who wins is the man who is on a first-name basis with the King.

Becoming a champion can be dangerous or scary to some of us. Those around you can wonder if the changes in you are for real. They might think, 'Can this be true, that he's a new man.' Yes it can! It did in me, so why not you if you need to?

If you've been brought up with constant abuse and being called an idiot or a d—head, and you've never felt or acted like you're any good, you may have even come to believe you are useless and hopeless and won't amount to anything. You can hate yourself and not really know it.

Then it's time to draw a line in the sand and remember and consider a couple of little sayings that help me: 'inch by inch is a cinch, yard by yard is too hard'. Little by little as things come up, name them, deal with them, confess them, and get freedom towards becoming a champion. **Bit-by-bit it will happen, and you will inspire other blokes with your life.** Take the step into champion freedom.

Champions clean out the gunk

The whole guts of the ministry of men is this: 'If you have sinned, you should tell each other what you have done. Then you can pray for one another and be healed' (James 5:16 in the *Work Manual*).

I say that to all men everywhere. **Spill your guts. Get rid of all this gunk inside you. Get sorted out** so you can be the real-deal champion you've been created to be. To whatever degree you want to get up there and spill it, you're going to be healed. This is the promise of it.

If men are in a safe non-judgemental place, they'll say, 'Yeah, I've stuffed it up.' Come up and come clean.

One of my close mates and I were having a chat about his battles. He kept beating around the bush and giving me the type of answers a politician would give. I didn't accept them. I said, 'Did you stuff it up?' Finally he said, 'Yeah, I did stuff it up.' It was like a huge weight being lifted off his shoulders.

Don't make hard work of this. **When you know you've stuffed something up, say sorry.** And even if the person doesn't want to accept sorry, you say sorry, because otherwise it will eat you out like cancer. Unforgiveness is like cancer.

If the person you need to say sorry to is dead or you can't get in touch with them, at least say sorry to the Big Fella about the whole issue.

I thank my Creator for showing me the battles where I've blown it. I say to him, 'Please forgive me for offending you. I'm a dirty, rotten, low-down, forgiven and loved sinner. But can we get on with it now Lord? Is it all over? Is it true you'll give the old blackboard a bit of a wipe and give me another go?' **And he sure gives you another chance.**

I spend many hours chatting with and listening to men all over the country. This is at the heart of a lot of their battles. Don't go trying to make hard work of it – keep it simple. Say sorry, ask for forgiveness, and get on with it. There might be more from the other person in time, but in the meantime you've gotta do what you've gotta do – say sorry.

Champions come to know the Big Fella on a first-name basis

True champions are just downright good and great human beings to be around because of who they are and Whose they are – they belong to their Creator. **It's a pleasure to meet a free and open man.** He accepts this champion's freedom from the old way to the new way of life. He continues to enjoy new freedom in his life and is great company for all around him.

Small changes within the heart of a bloke can make the largest differences for the better of all concerned. From little things, big things grow.

In the Creator's eyes the so-called down-and-outers of society, the unloved, the lost, the outcast can be given a new hope and a future and emerge the gemstones in his Kingdom. **Knowing him on a one-to-one basis, they can get a complete heart transformation without stitches.** They are now firmly entrenched in this champions' team after asking the Creator of the universe to give them an inside job for a new heart.

Champions, let's not point the finger

Take care as you become real. Let us never misuse our position or power to disadvantage others. We should not need to be judgemental, running around saying, 'You're wrong, you're wrong, you're wrong!' when we think someone else is heading in the wrong direction.

We need to begin by showing Jesus' love and the Creator's grace. We don't want someone to say, 'No, I'm not going to belong to the Big Fella because all his people want to do is come down here and tell me what I'm doing wrong.'

It's always best if we can get alongside the person who is in a doubtful situation. We might go and talk to the bloke and say, 'I don't think what you're doing is in the best interests of everybody and I can't agree with your actions. Could you reconsider what you're doing?'

Then if the person decides to change his ways, he will appreciate the way he was treated by you when you came alongside him. If you judge him he is more likely to put up a wall against what you believe.

Being a champion son of the King helps bring peace and calm to tense and pressured situations. You'll be the bloke who can go to the heart of the problem and ask those who offend to reconcile the consequences of their actions. Not by might or by power, but by the King's Spirit you can empower situations, and win the favour of other people.

The take-home message

You can do it. The champion team is ready for you. Are you ready to rise above and soar into the champion team? Take the freedom promised!

So I hope that you have enjoyed our great journey together in this book and are happily becoming that real-deal champion. I hope you have enjoyed every challenge, battle and adventure.

These chapters have covered some areas that I have firsthand knowledge of and I hope that they can help you in champion bloke battles that are of a similar nature. **There's nothing in this book that I haven't worked through in my life.** I hope that I have put it in everyday bloke's lingo so it brings past and present issues alive in your own battle.

If you can relate to it in your challenges and battles, you can now see victories and solutions. Remember don't just

A real-deal champion –
I am who I am, and I know Whose I am!

look at the dot on the page, look at the whole page for the big picture.

If you ever feel like you are in a 'prison', you could look at the bars and stop there. Or you could look out and see that beautiful blue sky and the stars at night or the moon coming over. You can start to see the stars and not the bars. Enjoy the happy and the good, and handle the sad and the bad.

So onward and upwards and rip into enjoying who you are and every minute of your life. The Creator said to his boy Jesus, 'You are my boy and I am well pleased with you.' In other words: 'Jesus, you are OK and you are my Champion'.

He says the same to each of us blokes: 'You are my boy and you're OK.'

I hope you can now hear it and believe it and get on with being a real and true champion and enjoy every moment and person in your life.

All the best!

Every bloke's a champion, even you!

TO REMEMBER...

Congratulations! You are now enjoying:

1. Receiving and giving empowering turbocharged words
2. Dreaming your dreams
3. Conquering hatred, bitterness, resentment, judgement and unforgiveness
4. Listening and hearing
5. Knowing the Big Fella on a first name basis
6. Sorting out any and all issues with your mother and your father
7. Strong and open trust
8. Dealing with anger
9. Both directional and nurture love in good balance
10. Appreciating what loving sex is
11. Giving and receiving generously
12. A new and open heart.

Enjoy your journey. See you in the truck or the shed.

Love ya guts,

Watto

www.ingramcontent.com/pod-product-compliance
Lightning Source LLC
LaVergne TN
LVHW051548070426
835507LV00021B/2475